GROVE PRESS MODERN DRAMATISTS

Grove Press Modern Dramatists
Series Editors: *Bruce King* and *Adele King*

Published titles

Eugene Benson, *J. M. Synge*
Normand Berlin, *Eugene O'Neill*
Denis Calandra, *New German Dramatists*
Neil Carson, *Arthur Miller*
Ruby Cohn, *New American Dramatists, 1960–1980*
Bernard F. Dukore, *Harold Pinter*
Frances Gray, *John Arden*
Julian Hilton, *Georg Büchner*
Charles R. Lyons, *Samuel Beckett*
Susan Bassnett-McGuire, *Luigi Pirandello*
Leonard C. Pronko, *Eugène Labiche and Georges Feydeau*
Theodore Shank, *American Alternative Theatre*
Nick Worrall, *Nikolai Gogol and Ivan Turgenev*

Further titles in preparation

GROVE PRESS MODERN DRAMATISTS

NEW GERMAN DRAMATISTS

A Study of Peter Handke,
Franz Xaver Kroetz,
Rainer Werner Fassbinder,
Heiner Müller,
Thomas Brasch,
Thomas Bernhard
and
Botho Strauss

Denis Calandra

Associate Professor
Department of Theatre
University of South Florida
Tampa, Florida

Grove Press, Inc., New York

First published in 1983 by
THE MACMILLAN PRESS LTD.
London and Basingstoke

First Hardcover Edition 1983
First Printing 1983
ISBN: 0-394-53499-9
Library of Congress Catalog Card Number: 83-48310

First Evergreen Edition 1983
First Printing 1983
ISBN: 0-394-62487-4
Library of Congress Catalog Card Number: 83-48310

Library of Congress Cataloging in Publication Data

Calandra, Denis.
   New German dramatists.

   (Grove Press modern dramatists)
   Includes index.
   Bibliography: p.
   1. German drama--20th century--History and
criticism. 2. German drama--Austrian authors--
History and criticism. I. Title. II. Series.
PT666.C36 1983   832'.914'09   83-48310
ISBN 0-394-53499-9
ISBN 0-394-62487-4 (pbk.)

Printed in the United States of America

GROVE PRESS, INC., 196 West Houston Street,
New York, N.Y., 10014

5 4 3 2 1

Contents

13919

List of Plates

1. *Rotter* by Thomas Brasch. A scene from the premiere in 1977 directed by Christof Nel with sets by Karl Ernst Hermann.
    Photo: Abisag Tüllman.
2. and 3. *Minetti* by Thomas Bernhard. Bernhard Minetti in the title role. Directed by Claus Peymann, Stuttgart, 1976.
    Photo: Abisag Tüllman.
4. *Der Auftrag* (*The Mission*) by Heiner Müller with Jürgen Holz as Debuisson. Directed by Heiner Müller and Ginka Tscholakowa at the Theater im dritten Stock in East Berlin in 1981.
    Photo: Willy Saeger.
5. *Gross und Klein* (*Big and Little*) by Botho Strauss. Edith Clever as Lotte. Directed by Peter Stein in Berlin in 1979.
    Photo: Ruth Walz.
6. *Heimarbeit* (*Homework*) by Franz Xaver Kroetz from the premiere at the Werkraumtheater, Munich

in 1971. Directed by Horst Seide.
Photo: Hildegard Steinmetz.
7. and 8. *Die Wahl fürs Leben* (*The Choice for Life*) by
Franz Xaver Kroetz at the Munich Theater Rechts
der Isar, in 1980.
9. The set of *Nicht Fisch, Nicht Fleisch* (*Neither Fish
nor Fowl*). Directed by Peter Stein in Berlin in 1981.
Photo: Ruth Walz.
10. *Kaspar* by Peter Handke. Directed by Peter Brook
with the Centre International de Recherche
Théâtrale. Presented in penal institutions on the
outskirts of Paris in 1972.
Photo: Nicolas Tikhomiroff.
11. *Ritt über den Bodensee* (*The Ride across Lake
Constance*). Directed by Claus Peymann and
Wolfgang Wiens.
Photo: Abisag Tüllman.
12. *Der anachronistiche Zuq* (*Procession of
Anachronisms*) by Bertolt Brecht. Hanne Hiob
Brecht in the background.

Note on translation
To facilitate the study of available texts in translation the
standard published English versions of the plays have been
quoted and are listed in the bibliography. All other
translations are by the author.

Acknowledgements

I would like to thank the Division of Sponsored Research and the College of Fine Arts of the University of South Florida for travel and study grants which enabled me to complete this book. In addition I would like to express my gratitude to my colleagues in the Department of Theatre, and to Betty Falcone Lichtenberg for her endless secretarial and research assistance. The interviews and direct information about current German theatre practice in this book come largely due to the kindness of German theatre workers, too many to enumerate, to whom I have spoken here and abroad. Thank you. I would also like to express my gratitude to Sue-Ellen Case, Helen Fehervary, Marc D. Silberman for their translation of *Cement*, and to Catherine Jelski for her translation of *Lovely Rita*. Finally, a word of thanks to my wife and children, who put up with me.

Editors' Preface

The *Grove Press Modern Dramatists* is an international series of introductions to major and significant nineteenth and twentieth century dramatists, movements and new forms of drama in Europe, Great Britain, America and new nations such as Nigeria and Trinidad. Besides new studies of great and influential dramatists of the past, the series includes volumes on contemporary authors, recent trends in the theatre and on many dramatists, such as writers of farce, who have created theatre 'classics' while being neglected by literary criticism. The volumes in the series devoted to individual dramatists include a biography, a survey of the plays, and detailed analysis of the most significant plays, along with discussion, where relevant, of the political, social, historical and theatrical context. The authors of the volumes, who are involved with theatre as playwrights, directors, actors, teachers and critics, are concerned with the plays as theatre and discuss such matters as performance, character interpretation and staging, along with themes and contexts.

To the memory of my mother Joan Cogan Calandra; and to my father, Philip Calandra

1
Introduction

Wolf Biermann, the East German poet and singer now living in the West, opened the decade of the eighties with a poem in the 11 January 1980 issue of *Die Zeit* dedicated to his late friend Rudi Dutschke, the radical who, he says, was 'a little too gentle like all genuine radicals'. Dutschke had recently succumbed to the lingering effects of three gunshot wounds sustained during the days of the student movement a dozen years before, when he was a popular hero of the rebellious post-World War II generation in Germany. 'Those were wide open days!', Biermann writes, 'That was in sixty eight, when it all got started with Vietnam/and with the murderer, the Shah.' Dutschke died in his bathtub, not on the barricades; and as we now know, the void left by the Shah was not exactly filled with enlightenment. Symptomatically for the decade of the seventies, Biermann forced his public anger through a nostalgic private sorrow, promising Dutschke that the 'real murderers', not just the hapless individual who wielded the Colt, would 'not be forgotten'.

1

In Germany, as elsewhere in the West, the advent of a new decade in 1980 triggered numerous reassessments of developments since 1968, when radical change seemed right around the corner. An illustration of directions in recent German theatre could be an outline for a parable by Bertolt Brecht, and includes his real-life daughter, Hanne Hiob, and his son, Stefan. The quite different 'radical' pursuits they were following at the turn of the decade represent opposite ends of the spectrum within which most of the important theatre and drama took place. Hanne Hiob Brecht, a professional actress who had played Johanna Dark in Gustav Gründgen's 1959 production of *St. Joan of the Stockyards*, was active in a monumental piece of street theatre which toured dozens of West German cities leading up to the federal elections in October 1980. Based on her father's poem, *The Procession of Anachronisms* (itself based on a Shelley poem), the piece attacked candidate F. J. Strauss of the right-wing CDU/CSU (Christian Democratic Union/Christian Social Union) and warned of a gradual reinstatement of fascist leadership in West Germany under private capitalism. When I asked about her work, she said 'The people are very responsive to our performance wherever we go. This is the kind of theatre which today is of the first importance. Brecht would have approved. It carries on his tradition.'

By contrast, Stefan Brecht, son of the playwright, was busy at the end of the decade writing a 440-page book on the theatre of Robert Wilson, entitled *The Theatre of Visions*, in which he analyses the work of the influential American artist, and darling of the European *avant-garde*. Wilson's striking universe of theatrical images begins and ends with the imagination, implying a revolution inside the head as the only viable one. 'I am not interested in changing the world through theatre', Wilson says, 'I'm giving people invitations to daydreams.' One is reminded of the famous expressions chalked on the wall of the Paris Opera in 1968: 'Be a realist. Ask for the impossible. Power to imagination.'

In the forties, Arthur Adamov was at the centre of the European *avant-garde*, writing absurdist texts; in the fifties he became engaged politically, a leading polemicist for Brecht against Ionesco; in 1970 he committed suicide. The critic Georg Hensel sees Adamov's death as 'sealing the end of the absurd theatre and signalling the agony of the political theatre.'[1] The absurd and the political; the private and the polemical: these are terms which define dramatic literature and theatrical production in Germany in the post-sixties period.

The most significant German language drama and theatre of the past fifteen years exists between these extremes. At one pole are the realists and activists, who, like Franz Xaver Kroetz, assume that the world can be understood, can be reproduced on stage in a multitude of forms, and productively changed. There is a root skepticism evident in others like Peter Handke for whom traditional notions of realism have lost all credibility. These writers are interested in perceived phenomena and feelings; their chief aim has a romantic cast to it as they ponder the mysteries of consciousness and attempt to create themselves anew by creating alternative worlds in artistic forms. Their attitude towards audiences seems to be: 'take it or leave it', whereas the former group are implicitly instructive, or at least concerned with setting rational mechanisms in motion for their audiences. In a television debate broadcast in 1977 Peter Handke accused Franz Xaver Kroetz of demagoguery and of wanting to put the world into a communist straitjacket, 'where no one would be able to breathe anymore'; and all this in the name of liberation. Kroetz in his turn decried artists like Handke as narcissists, poetical lackeys of the system which supports them, and incapable of responsibility to anything beyond their own egos. Nevertheless, both Handke and Kroetz, 'ivory tower resident' and Communist Party member respectively, used the familiar 'du' form of address, and more significantly they joined to attack the television programme moderator when he offered the 'independent' judgment that Kroetz was strident in his political pronouncements. Typically, Handke and Kroetz are united in their opposition to the prevailing order, though their temperaments lead them up very different paths.

Handke would defend Kroetz's right to oppose, though he considers his style of writing old fashioned depending as it does on empathy, a 'nineteenth century' phenomenon. Kroetz clearly values Handke's power through inventive formal techniques to expose the sources of human relationships, though he thinks it stops short of laying blame on the dominant capitalist system. When I asked him which playwrights are important to him, Kroetz did not hesitate to name Samuel Beckett, along with Athol Fugard and early Edward Bond. Beckett, who directed landmark productions of *Endgame* (1968) and *Waiting for Godot* (1975) in Berlin, has had a salient effect on the most diverse group of German writers and theatre artists. His broad influence indicates the difficulty of defining parameters of form and idea in contemporary German language drama. Beckett is no less important to Marxists like Kroetz or Heiner Müller than to Handke or Thomas Bernhard. In his excellent book, *Modern German Drama*, C. D. Innes traces in detail the German roots of 'a specifically contemporary stage vocabulary' through the work of Brecht, Dürrenmatt, Frisch and others.[2] In this short survey of representative playwrights I have set up an axis along broadly defined romantic and realistic views of reality and art, with the understanding that the greatest interest resides where the orientations and beliefs of the authors overlap.

As the period covered by this book dates roughly from the cultural tidewater mark of the late sixties, and as the theatre is by its nature a public and social art, underscored by the traditional German view of the (highly subsidized) stage as a tribunal where issues of importance are debated, some words on intellectual climate and artistic trends are in order.

The 'extra-parliamentary opposition' (APO – *ausserparlamentarische Opposition*) which coalesced in the late sixties in Germany to provide a counterforce to a threateningly monolithic middle of the road political alignment had not entirely disappeared in the seventies, but it had undergone considerable change. The intelligentsia and the student movement sought alternatives to the varieties of regimentation perceived in the prevailing social orders, but the social and political retrenchment of the seventies in Germany as elsewhere caused splintering among cultural and political alignments. Common cause still existed in opposition to repressive measures such as the *Berufsverbot* – the official black-balling of 'extremists', largely left-wing intellectuals, in teaching, law and government service. But resistance had its greatest effect not in practical spheres, but rather as a constant reminder of Germany's awful recent history in which small capitulations led to outright tyranny.

The most notorious reaction to Germany's reinstatement of order (*Ordnung*) after the sixties unrest came from the Red Army Faction, led by Ulrike Meinhof and Andreas Baader. Meinhof was engaged in the sixties as a social worker among the youthful human flotsam, by-products of West Germany's economic abundance. Frustration was no doubt one cause of her direct violent attacks in the seventies on the institutions of West German capitalism. There was something hopelessly romantic in the Baader/Meinhof escapades, however, and they were criticized by many as playing into the hands of those with the highest stake in the *status quo*. The issue of radical social change remained in focus due partly to the brutally real gestures of the Red Army Faction. Numerous theatres produced doctored versions of classic plays with revolutionary themes (Schiller's *The Robbers* being a favourite) some even showing open sympathy for the terrorists. Public debate and national tension grew with the capture, conviction and the deaths in prison, reputedly by suicide, of Andreas Baader, the group's leader, and two others, then it peaked with the dispute over their burial in the same respectable Frankfurt cemetery where a victim of terrorism had recently been interred. That was in 1977; by the early eighties the Red Army Faction had revived its systematic violence and was sharing publicity with increasingly brazen neo-fascist groups.

Perhaps to non-Germans the best known dramatic example of the mood at the time is to be found in the film, made collectively by Fassbinder, Schlöndorff and others, *Germany in Autumn* (1977). One particular scene, written by Heinrich Böll depicts a board meeting at which a major West German television network decides it is inexpedient, in view of the furor over the recent burial, to broadcast *Antigone*, as planned.[3] Böll's scene is invented, but not far-fetched, and it captures an air of lingering late sixties opposition spirit. Creon has a corporate face in Böll's scene, and his chief means of control is indirect ownership

6

of the means of communication. This film typifies an attempt by many writers to expose existing structures of control and to spur alternatives to what Hans Magnus Enzensberger has called the 'consciousness industry', the current media and information network which naturally supports the ruling order. In one way or another it could be said that all the writers discussed in this book are *de facto* opponents of that consciousness industry, regardless of their declared politics. Some of them, most successfully Kroetz and Fassbinder, have also attempted to penetrate the media and use its own aesthetic forms in radio and television to present alternative ideas.

As with Hanne Hiob Brecht in 1980 some artists continued the direct combination of theatre and reality in the streets. One uncannily effective activist who exploits the theatricality of the everyday for political purposes is Günter Wallraff. Wallraff had managed to smuggle himself into the upper echelons of power and ingratiate himself to such an extent that he could later publicly expose the realities of the power structure in the state. A typical Wallraff routine occurred when he disguised himself as a novice monk thereby gaining entry into the monastery of Father Emmeram, of the fabulously wealthy Thurn and Taxis family, in Regensburg, Bavaria. After collecting information on the unholy alliance of nobility, church and capital in West Germany, he arranged his departure to have a purely theatrical, and whimsical, effect. He rigged a loudspeaker, 'with the voice of God', to address the good pastor Emmeram directly, admonishing him to change his ways, do penance, and turn over his monastery to those who needed homes – large families, guest workers (*Gastarbieter* – foreign imported labourers), students. The priest listened in shock, then predictably and comically responded: 'That wasn't God. God doesn't

speak like that.'⁴ Wallraff's marginally theatrical prank
had a serious purpose, and his acting, judging by the anger
it provoked, was convincing.

The interpenetration of reality and theatricality which
blossomed in the sixties during demonstrations and public
meetings was not lost on the playwrights. Though far
removed from Wallraff's Marxism, Peter Handke clarified
the fact that normal effective theatre pales by comparison
with the spectacle of a student seizing the microphone
from a professor in a lecture hall, or of a demonstrator
with child in arms making an active political protest. These
observations led Handke to a reassessment of the
aesthetics of theatrical form. When reality becomes more
and more theatrical, what happens to the theatre? Kroetz
took a different approach in assessing theatricality. A
favourite device of his is to show his characters observing
the 'world theatre' on television, in the form of
coronations, global politics and even celebrity talk shows,
while they themselves carry on unreflectingly day to day
with the social roles defined for them by those in positions
of power.

Another broad-based movement which gradually took
shape in the seventies has come to be known as the 'green'
revolution, a loose collection of artists, thinkers and
activists united in their opposition to the destruction of the
environment, the unchecked proliferation of nuclear
power, and blueprints for reality provided by dogmatic
political thinkers. A figurehead for this movement is Josef
Beuys, an artist, performer, teacher, who, together with
Heinrich Böll, formed in 1972 what they called the Free
International University to propagate their ideas. Beuys's
vision for the future in which 'every man is an artist' in a
system of 'free democratic socialism' has been an implicit
theme in most of his work. He is never too precise about

what 'free democratic socialism' means, however. For Beuys, violence is creative energy gone bad; and systematic repression of people by the 'consciousness industry' can only be checked by tapping the positive flow of energy in all people. Beuys's utopian imaginings have been attacked by many as either totally ineffectual and romantic, or as a great fraud perpetrated by the artist/guru who sells eccentric products masquerading as art to buyers interested primarily in novelty. Beuys was an important presence to Germany's alternative culture of the sixties and seventies, and a 'green' political party supported actively by him has seriously begun to campaign for office. Before he died, the 'gentle' revolutionary of Wolf Biermann's poem, the Marxist Rudi Dutschke, even expressed sentiments closer to Beuys's than to his own late sixties ideas. He advocated mobilizing 'popular support for an alternative to private and state capitalism', damning both sides of divided Germany.[5]

In another poem dedicated to the memory of Dutschke, this one written in 1981 by Heinrich Böll, the poet addresses himself directly and personally to Josef Beuys on the occasion of the artist's sixtieth birthday. He warns Beuys, in a friendly way, about the perils of fame, and implores him not to forget 'Rudi, Dutschke' and the fire of the late revolutionary, who is 'freezing, forgotten'. The process which started in the sixties was still undergoing the natural permutations of any cultural movement. The frequent public appearances of Beuys, teaching his ideas and embodying them in performances, acted as emblems reminding people of a spirit and an ideal of a not too distant past. Both the mood of the movement associated with Beuys and the specific qualities of his performance are of interest.

Peter Handke commented on a Beuys performance he

saw at the 'experimenta 3' festival in Frankfurt in 1969. What he had to say tells us something about his own work in relation to the innovative performance art of the sixties. The production co-directed by Claus Peymann was titled *Iphigenia/Titus Andronicus.* Peymann had directed Handke's first plays as well, and was to become an important maverick director in the seventies. He directed a play based on material written by Ulrike Meinhof, and because of overt sympathy for terrorists (money collected in his theatre to pay for their prison dental treatment for example) was eventually forced to leave his post in Stuttgart. Peymann has also been closely associated with Thomas Bernhard, a playwright who rejects all forms of direct political theatre.

In *Iphigenia/Titus Andronicus* two actors' voices reading patches from the Goethe and Shakespeare texts were piped in while Beuys in very amateur fashion, according to the approving Handke, spoke selections from *Iphigenia.* On stage with Beuys was a beautiful white horse which, he later explained, 'seemed to echo my expressions, as the photographs show'. The confrontation of civilized cultures represented by Shakespeare and Goethe in the presence of man and a pure natural beast, constituted Beuys's drama. Its mood was gentle, unhectic and typical of the 'green' alternative. Handke enthusiastically described the effect the performance had on him in terms reserved for only one other type of performance from the late sixties, the mythic pieces of the American Bread and Puppet Theatre. Since founding the Bread and Puppet Theatre in 1961 German born Peter Schumann and his associates have created performances based on a variety of sources including the Bible, ancient myth, and folk tales. Using puppets of different sizes as well as actors Schumann has developed a distinctive imagery as a way of expressing a need for humanistic values in the world. The Bread and Puppet Theatre sought unorthodox audiences outside normal theatre circuits and involved them in the productions in a unique manner, typically by distributing bread prior to performances which the company had baked itself. Handke writes of Beuys's experiment, 'But the further this event recedes in time the more strongly do the horse and the man moving on stage and the voices over the loudspeakers merge into an image that one might call ideal. In the memory it seems to have been fused into one's own life, an image that works through both nostalgia and the will to produce such images oneself: for it is only as an after-image that it really starts to work in one's mind.'[6]

The emphasis is decidedly on the individual's private imaginative capacity: the communication is by absorption of image, and distinctly non-rational. In a 1977 diary entry Handke compares himself to Brecht: 'To think naturalistic forms to ruins, until they yield the didactic, indicative (Brecht); to think didactic forms to ruins until they yield myths (my writing).' (*The Weight of the World*, p. 321)

Private insight and vision balanced against the need to oppose and protest against external pressures: this is a central dichotomy for writers of the past fifteen years. When a student wrote to explain his thinking to H. E. Richter, Professor of Psychosomatic Medicine at Giessen University – 'We are trying, by changing the external world, to save our inner-world' (*Die Zeit*, 3 July 1981) – he was echoing Böll's and Beuys's Free International University Manifesto of 1972: 'Environmental pollution advances parallel with a pollution of the world within us.' Peter Handke quotes the nineteenth-century novelist Jean Paul in a headnote to his collection of poems, *The Innerworld of the Outerworld of the Innerworld* (1969), '. . . your outer and your inner world are soldered together like the two halves of a shell and enclose you, the mollusc –', clearly aligning his own generation's inner/outer dichotomy to a larger tradition.

As a final note on shifting cultural trends one can look at the work of Max Frisch, whose native Switzerland some ten years late seems to be experiencing a youth rebellion of its own in the early eighties. When he was at the height of his popularity in the early sixties Frisch was considered to be in a direct line of descent from Bertolt Brecht. Between the early political parables like *The Fireraisers* and *Andorra* and his play of 1968 with the revealing title *Biography*, however, a significant shift had taken place along lines that were to be followed by others in the seventies. In an interview on 24 April 1981 in *Die Zeit* Frisch explained his own position as someone who finds the old political vocabulary 'and not just that of Marxists' to have outlived its usefulness. 'Right now I think texts which avoid direct political vocabulary', he says, 'are far more irritating, far more stimulating for the political consciousness of the reader, subversive in the best sense of the word.' Questioned about the subjective orientation of his recent writings, including the latest play, *Triptych*, Frisch bristled at the absurd notion that has been grinding its way along for the last thirteen years: that private is a dirty word (*Schreckwort*). For Frisch, who still devoutly wishes for such socialist transformations as public ownership of heavy industry and banks, the old ideas for achieving such changes seem outmoded. In artistic terms he has experimented in the forms of perception in drama. 'What has always fascinated me about theatre,' he says, 'is the confrontation of physical being (*Existenz*) and language.' This could almost be a statement by Peter Handke. Also typical of the seventies is Frisch's perception that the women's movement could have the potential to

12

bring about social changes, which as he points out could also bring about the emancipation of men. For someone of Max Frisch's stature to have said these things is an indication of altered moods and points of emphasis.

2
The Playwrights

This book is an introduction to German drama as represented by the Austrians Peter Handke and Thomas Bernhard; East Germans Heiner Müller and Thomas Brasch; and West Germans Franz Xaver Kroetz, Rainer Werner Fassbinder and Botho Strauss. For convenience the usual adjective 'German' will be used to describe the work of all the playwrights. Specifics of nationality will be dealt with where they add to an understanding of the work; for example, the linguistic and romantic tradition in Austria; regionalism in Kroetz; non-Western aspects of the East Germans' plays.

Peter Handke

Peter Handke, a vociferous, though independent participant in the sixties rebellion, soon turned away from polemics. *Kaspar*, his 'speech torture' play as he described it, had its premiere in 1968. It dealt with the systematic process of forcing the main figure, based on the legendary

Kaspar Hauser, to conformity with the social 'order' of things. Its emphasis on the theme of order (*Ordnung*) and repression proved it to be symptomatic of the thinking of the post-war generation, those born in the ruins and brought up into the German 'miracle'. Handke was born in 1942 and he describes the war as a 'childhood nightmare that would colour [his] whole emotional development'. His background is working-class Catholic. He spent five years in a seminary school, and later studied law for several years before his spectacular entry into the literary scene, 'theatricalizing' himself, as his critics noted, with the help of canny publishers, as a literary phenomenon. His formally experimental plays achieved a notoriety for him between 1965 and 1974, when the last play, *They Are Dying Out*, was produced. A recently published play, *Among the Villages* (1981), is yet to be produced. Handke's character Wilhelm Meister (based on the famous Goethe figure), in the Wim Wenders film which he scripted, *False Move* (1974), expresses with typical detachment what seems to be a seventies nostalgia for the previous decade: 'If only both of them, the poetical and political, could be unified.' The writer's elderly companion in the film responds: 'That would be the end of yearning (*Sehnsucht*) and the end of the world.' Handke's own careful yearning for a 'poetical' revolution, a very private desire to achieve clarity of thought and a mental harmony in which the emotions could function honestly and unaffectedly, seemed to many observers wildly out of touch with brutal seventies realities.

When one looks back, however, at a remarkable piece of theatre like Handke's *My Foot My Tutor* (1969) in which two figures deliberately mime a set of everyday rituals in an apparent master/slave relationship, and thinks about significant shifts in artistic and cultural temperament

15

which seem to have taken place in the recent past, one sees that the question of artistic sensibility and the responsibility of the writer to reflect external reality is more complicated than Handke's critics would allow. Violence was a fact in the sixties and seventies, apparent not just in terrorist exploits, but as an underlying social phenomenon. In divided Germany, one of the world's largest armed camps, this fact is perhaps more prominently influential than elsewhere. In their Manifesto for a Free International University Böll and Beuys wrote: 'Hope [in our world] is denounced as Utopia or as illusory, and discarded hope breeds violence. In the school we shall research into the numerous forms of violence, which are by no means confined to weapons or physical force.'[1]

My Foot My Tutor in part seems the result of Peter Handke's research into violence as a component of personal and social relationships. In the very 'cool' course of the action nothing extraordinarily shocking takes place, but the implied degree of violent energy is enormous; the playwright sets down very careful observations, gestures to be contemplated. In mood the piece could only result from the process of inner reflection on external reality. Handke's idea here, and in other works, has a precursor in the nineteenth century Austrian writer, Adalbert Stifter, according to whose 'gentle law' even the most trivial action or phenomenon can have enormous significance. Carefully observed, the pitcher of milk boiling over on the stove, for Stifter, can have the equivalent power of a mighty volcano The 'gentle law' is one of those chestnuts which would have appeared in literary school texts when Handke was young.

Handke's observations also correspond to Beuys's work in pieces like *Coyote* (1974), in which Beuys enacted a series of repeated rituals with a live coyote in front of an audience. An idea behind the piece performed in New York was to deal with 'the whole American trauma with the Indian, the Red Man'. Implicitly, of course, the performance deals with the dramatic and traumatic continuing saga of colonialism and of violence to environments: as Caroline Tisdall describes it, the performance seems to have corresponded in seriousness and in its 'quiet' personal method to the work of Handke and others in the seventies. Beuys wanted to confront the fact that 'there is no single language that can express the many levels of consciousness through which it is possible to perceive the totality of phenomena and entities', so he turned to a theatrical form.[2]

Amongst dramatists themselves there has been a turning to formal experiments not entirely unrelated to Beuys's work in spirit, which attempt to grapple with reality and with the many levels of consciousness through which it is perceived. What began as a Wittgensteinian investigation of verbal language evolved for Peter Handke to a concern with all of the sign systems of theatre, and of reality. The quieter, inner-directed work of Handke and others came to be known as the 'new sensibility' or 'new subjectivity' in the seventies. Characteristically, Handke noted the shift from 'political' to 'spontaneous-sensitive' among people on the 'cultural scene' in the seventies in his published journal, *The Weight of the World* (1977): 'There is simply no other way to get around these non-persons except with a punch in the face.' (p. 156). This is a curiously violent personal response to a shift in cultural mood by someone whose work is at the heart of that shift. But Handke is consistent in having helped create a trend, then being repelled by its becoming 'trendy'. His work remains sharply critical even of his own private reality, as the detached irony of his style attests.

Franz Xaver Kroetz

The Bavarian Franz Xaver Kroetz (born 1946), broadly describes his work as realistic. His deceptively simple plays recreate the rhythms of speech and the behaviour patterns of his fellow Bavarians, of 'ordinary' people from sub-proletarian to working-class and middle-class milieus, in order to present people in contemporary society with images of themselves as individual and social beings, so that they can clarify their state of existence in society and, by changing their consciousness, take steps to change the order of things in the world. The pressures of economics, moral habit, fixed modes of thinking have been his themes. The violence of everyday life showed itself in his early work in subjects like abortion, infanticide, rape, but the pace of the action was such that the spectacular aspects of the deeds were played down in favour of a mood of reflection on the 'why' of the occurrences. Kroetz's concern that he be understood by a mass audience leads him to be rather conservative in form, though his plays are by no means simple. In Kroetz's introduction to *Request Concert* we find the social causes of a suicide underscored, but not explicitly in the text. In that play a lonely middle-aged woman mimes her evening routine and then matter-of-factly destroys herself with an overdose of pills. There is nothing spectacular in the play, but it is as penetrating a comment on mundane violence as any piece of theatre by his contemporaries.

As the playwright whose work was most frequently produced in the seventies, and who has made inroads into television and radio, Kroetz proudly asserted when I spoke to him in 1980 that the trend toward 'new subjectivity' (the work of Handke, Strauss, Bernhard and others) does not mean that the time 'for us realists has passed'. He mentioned that his plays are now set texts for school children in many state schools, and, on a personal note, he read from a letter he had received from a seventeen-year-old girl which quaintly confirmed for himself the success he is after. The girl begins with an expression of humility, nervously wondering if it is even appropriate to write to an eminent playwright, then goes on to thank him for the play *Mensch Meier* she had just seen, claiming its depiction of reality was 'just like at home', and that it helped her to come to grips with her situation.

Kroetz was not an activist in the late sixties; rather he was an occasional day labourer, and intermittently employed as an actor. He had also done some writing and acting for a Bauerntheater – low-level dinner-theatre that specializes in farce and various entertainment skits. Kroetz had early experiences with the work of Marieluise Fleisser, the author whose realistic plays about provincial life in Bavaria had, along with the earlier revival of plays by Ödön von Horváth (*Tales of the Vienna Woods*), been part of a revival of the folk-play genre in the sixties. These plays were very different from the polemical Brecht revivals, and in tone far removed from the collection of documentary pieces by Hochhuth, Weiss and others which were paramount in the sixties. Their appeal lay in the simplicity of realistic form and the immediate accessibility, as well as the seriousness with which they exposed the miserable lot of ordinary, usually middle or working class provincials, in the era of the Weimar Republic. Kroetz was also working at the Münchner Kammerspiele while Edward Bond's *Saved* was being produced in 1968, in a translation from South London slang to a stylized Munich street talk by Martin Sperr. Kroetz still admires this work of Bond's, though the later, more 'poetical' pieces like *Lear*, he finds too abstruse.

After he had already been acclaimed as an important new writer with successes like *Stallerhof, Request Concert, Homework* and others, Kroetz's response to the waning of the 'opposition' in the seventies was to join the German Communist Party (legalized in 1968). In his essay 'Socialism Out of a Love for Reason', he claims the search for socialist alternatives derived from a mixture of Christian compassion for the underprivileged and the conviction that only on a mass organized scale could things be changed. 'I'd very much like to be happy, but as long as others are suffering I find it impossible.'[3] His idea of realism, which 'places the normal working human being at the centre of artistic creation', could only be coupled with close association with the organizations of the working class, 'best of all with our German Communist Party'.[4] Kroetz's choice to bind himself politically in this way ran counter to the trend among intellectuals and artists, though people like Günter Grass continued in active support of the Social Democratic Party, which has been in power since the early seventies. In some of his plays Kroetz tried to introduce 'positive' directions of a socialist realist stamp, though he managed to avoid simply mouthing party formulas in all but the consciously agit-prop pieces of the seventies.

It seems unfair that Kroetz should have been accused by the Party newspaper of succumbing to the 'green mode' when he decided in May 1980 to withdraw from Communist Party membership, though there is a hint of that in his statement of resignation. The reasons he gave were: finding the Social Democrats on the whole more sympathetic; disagreement with certain features of socialism as he knew it (presumably in East Germany); inability to subscribe to the customary Marxist belief in progress, especially where it concerns questions of the relationship of human beings to their environment. For Kroetz the advent of a new decade meant a need for a new kind of opposition, not to his former party, not in the direction of the gentle anarchists Beuys and the greens, but as an independent Marxist. In his recent play, *Neither Fish Nor Fowl* (1980), the story of a redundant type-setter, the problem of women's emancipation is an important theme.

Fassbinder

Early in the seventies, Rainer Werner Fassbinder, a fellow Bavarian, known outside of Germany largely for his films, expressed sympathies similar to those of Kroetz's, though from the start he showed a temperamental disinclination to engage in anyone else's party politics. Like Kroetz, Fassbinder was influenced by the folk play revival, and had a hand in encouraging the tendency himself with a production in 1969 of Fleisser's *Pioneers in Ingolstadt* in which Kroetz played the part of a young officer. Though he has not written many plays, Fassbinder merits some attention in this book because of his enormous creative output and influence, and not least because he is likely to be well known to English-speaking audiences. When I asked Kroetz about his own work he explained that he does not just think of the theatre; his province rather is the entire area of *Drama*, which includes theatre, film, television and radio. And so it is for Fassbinder, whose work for the stage and in other media overlaps in so many ways, formally and otherwise. By studying Fassbinder's films one can acquire a feeling for concrete features of recent German drama not available in any other way to those not privileged to see stage productions in their country of origin. Fassbinder's plays, some of which have been reworked into films, and his work on specific television serials, are useful reference points when discussing dramatic styles. Because of the maverick approach to form and idea and his eclectic body of work he also acts as a kind of barometer for the German cultural scene.

Typically, in the film *Germany in Autumn*, Fassbinder's section, which includes himself, his mother and his late-male-lover in the cast, deals with a very personal despair and rage, a feeling that universal collapse is imminent, that the inner wheels and outer wheels have ground to a halt, a sharp contrast to Böll/Schlöndorff's satirical *Antigone* section.

Heiner Müller

The other committed Marxist to be treated in this book is the older East German playwright Heiner Müller (born 1929). His work has undergone radical changes since his first play appeared in 1956. In his early efforts he attempted to retain a critical stance towards the East German reality he was depicting while keeping within the bounds of socialist realist dogma. His more recent work has a more visionary mythical dimension, combining in increasingly fragmentary texts an Artaudian intensity with a deep commitment to trying to understand his country's brutally contradictory history.

Müller's work never completely removes the historical dimension, as do the playwrights of the 'new subjectivity', but his own struggle with the idea of revolution, its hopes, contradictions and failures seems at times to be a series of individual nightmares based on haunting historical realities. The tone of Müller's work is quite different from that of Handke's or others. Müller's use of extreme brutality, including cannibalism, which raises the hackles of some critics, of course had its equivalent in Nazi reality. Müller continues to remind Germans of that specific reality. A chronicle of mass-murder trials in *Die Zeit* (17 July 1981) reproduced the Treblinka camp testimony about the commandant Franz and his mongrel St Bernard, Barry. 'The witness described how Franz set his Barry on a naked prisoner and how Barry bit off the man's sex organ, and how another time, urged on by Franz, he tore out a piece of flesh from a prisoner.' This is the background for Müller's imagery.

Müller's perspective on the idea of 'revolution betrayed' doesn't derive from the euphoria of the late sixties, but rather from commitment to the work of constructing a socialist alternative based on the Soviet model. Like most East German artists Müller was at first received in the West as something of an exotic, but the plays produced in the seventies in the Federal Republic offer a constant challenge, from experience, to ideas, utopian and otherwise, which were generated by the sixties opposition and which continue to haunt the German intelligentsia. Müller's images of brutality in the face of brutality, and of hope deferred for a better future, framed into poetic wholes of a unique kind, balance the inner-directed works of serious seventies playwrights in German-speaking countries. Müller's are the most intense reflections of divided Germany. He paraphrases Edgar Allen Poe in the headnote to one volume of plays, *Germania Death in Berlin*: – 'The terror of which I write does not come from Germany. It is a terror of the soul.' Müller adds to this: 'The terror of which I write comes from Germany'. A Brechtian influence is evident, to the point where Müller claims that 'Brecht uncriticized is Brecht betrayed.' He frequently cites Antonin Artaud and Samuel Beckett as sources of inspiration as well. The presentation of social, human contradictions, and the personal grappling with the themes of violence and revolution produce highly poetic and evocative scenes. The flavour of performance of his most successful pieces bears greater similarity to the anarchic imaginings of the Middle European grotesque tradition – Witkiewicz, Kantor, Szajna – than to Brecht's learning plays or his later parables.

Thomas Brasch

Unlike Müller, Thomas Brasch (born 1945) has chosen to emigrate to West Germany, where his imagistic personal plays and his first film, *Iron Angel* (1981), have received considerable attention. Inevitably for an East German writer the problem of accommodating aesthetic and political pressures has been a concern of Brasch's. Interviewed by *Die Zeit* (8 May 1981), he refused to be drawn into commenting on his apparent lack of direct political involvement. He had been incarcerated in East Berlin because of his views, and in 1980 he had signed a letter along with Günter Grass and others protesting against the trend toward nuclear armament in the West, specifically the placing of additional missiles on West German soil. Pressed to explain his attitude as a writer in difficult political times, Brasch gave an answer close to Handke's and others like him. He cannot see the point, he says, in active political participation because even a critical stance toward the state denotes participation in the state. Most of what officials have to say, he claims, has nothing to do with him personally; he had learned the futility of such exercises. All states, any state system, is narrowing and limiting to the individual. Brasch's plays, nevertheless, deal with historical and political material. The figure of Georg Heym in his *Lieber Georg* (1979) is typical. The early pacifist expressionist poet's terrifying visions became reality after 1914, and the play shows him in the vortex of personal and historical conditions he cannot control, but only feel. The structure of Brasch's play itself is fragmentary, poetically suggestive. In another play, *Lovely Rita*, the central figure is placed in Berlin at 'zero hour', after the collapse, but the focus of the play is the effect of wartime and post-war disintegration on the individual. Brasch's sensibility, along with Handke's and Strauss's, turns to private agonies.

Botho Strauss

In 1970 Botho Strauss (born 1944) stated the need to find a way 'to combine the aesthetic and the political'. His work as a critic for *Theater heute*, the most influential German language theatre journal, and his association as dramaturg with the Schaubühne am Halleschen Ufer (Berlin) during its politically assertive days in the early seventies, gave him more than the other playwrights treated in this book a position from which to approach the theatre and its relation to German reality analytically. Under Peter Stein's direction the Schaubühne mounted influential productions and engaged in its own 'social experiment' of *Mitbestimmung* (worker participation) in the organization of the institution. Full participation and discussion of particulars of programmes and productions was extended to members of staff not normally consulted. That Peter Stein's voice was usually followed, according to critic Peter Iden, doesn't detract from the fact that the 'collective' atmosphere produced superior work.[5] Strauss's work with Stein on widely acclaimed productions of *Peer Gynt* (1971) and *Summerfolk* (1973) newly defined the role of dramaturg in the German theatre as actual production collaborator rather than as the more common peripheral consultant. Strauss's extensive work on Gorky's *Summerfolk*, which toured Great Britain in 1974, gives an insight into his own plays. As in the Gorky piece, Strauss's characters tend to be forlorn, lost, useless human beings, pathetic in the fragility of their feelings and their inability to escape the pointless repetition in their daily lives and the stagnation which will ultimately envelop them. In *Summerfolk* the new class of working people was ready to sweep away the debris, whereas in Strauss's own plays no such hope looms in the future.

The pressures of society are felt indirectly in the steady disruption of mental stability of Strauss's individual characters. *Big and Little*, acclaimed as the best new work of 1978, has at its core the mental agonies of an alienated woman facing middle age. The final scene finds the woman, Lotte, alone, disturbed, waiting in a doctor's antechamber. The absurd aging students (relics of the sixties), guest-workers and others who share the landscape of the play with her are part of West German reality, but the emphasis, in expressionist style, is decidedly on the private. There is no introduction, as in Kroetz's *Request Concert*, in which one reads a social critique. Peter Iden notes a parallel between changes in the Schaubühne am Halleschen Ufer, which opened the seventies with a production of Brecht's polemical *The Mother* and went on to stress plays like *Big and Little*, and the changing current in Germany at large. Botho Strauss, registering his detachment with irony (in *Trilogy of Reunions* he sets his intelligent, sensitive characters against the backdrop of an art exhibit with the title 'Capitalist Realism'), is a young playwright and novelist in the independent tradition of Peter Handke, yearning for some inner harmony, skeptical of ever attaining it.

The Playwrights

Thomas Bernhard

The Austrian Thomas Bernhard (born 1931) won a reputation as a novelist in the sixties and only had his first play produced in 1971. Since then he has given vent to his consistent idiosyncratic vision in a steady output of plays about the futility of all human endeavour in the face of death. His particular experience of war and its aftermath, chronicled in semi-autobiographical novels, has led him to a general despair. Unlike his contemporary Heiner Müller he sees no redeeming possibilities in the force of history. The idea of revolution or any widespread change for the better is one among many human pretensions in Bernhard's absurdist texts. The characteristic monologues in his plays embody the obsessive ramblings of people in extreme states of consciousness: a 'persecuted' former Nazi officer; a circus director compelled to master Schubert's *Trout Quintet*; a crabby intellectual, the 'world-improver' of one play. It is no wonder that the director, Claus Peymann, who first produced Handke's experimental plays, has also become the chief exponent of Bernhard's work, for both Austrians share a concern with the purely linguistic features of their dramas, to the neglect of conventional plot and rounded character.

Bernhard has carefully controlled the production rights of his plays, indicating an awareness that his theatre pieces need special handling by specific actors and directors. As for thematic material, aside from a tendency to. view the creation of artistic fictions as preferable to 'reflecting the world as it is' and a certain shared bitter humour, Bernhard and Handke differ considerably. Bernhard has remarked that Handke's yearning for 'harmony' in relationships and his expressed hope in individual poetical 'revolutions' is nothing short of sentimental. Bernhard

27

stands alone in the contemporary German theatre scene, prolifically issuing Jeremiads to the public which comes to his plays.

The playwrights have tried to come to grips with objective facts of repression and the inner turmoil it engenders, some trying to tap new sources of harmony and emotional freedom within, others playing out the dialectic between felt emotions and rationally understood courses of opposition, and have created an impressive body of drama. There is a seriousness about the theatre in Germany which, though it can and often does descend to tedious solemnity, does set it apart at its best moments from theatre elsewhere. It is this seriousness of intent which unites all of the plays to be considered, whether the actual tone of the product be bloody farce or disguised modern morality play. A ruling principle for the playwrights as well as for anyone who would study them could be that written by Hans Magnus Enzensberger in 1962 in his essay on the *avant-garde:* 'The law of increasing reflection is inexorable. Whoever tries to dodge it ends up offered for sale at a discount by the consciousness industry.'[6] In 1981 Ralf Dahrendorf, the expert on German politics and society, and Administrator of the London School of Economics, together with other observers of the German cultural scene, were already talking of a revival of the sixties 'opposition' mood. The playwrights, along with other artists, in keeping with the 'law of increasing reflection' in their various ways, were at the heart of that movement.

3
Kroetz and Handke: A Comparison

To introduce the theatre of Peter Handke and Franz Xaver Kroetz it may be useful to make a comparative analysis of Handke's mime play *My Foot My Tutor* (1969) and three Kroetz plays – *The Choice For Life* (1973/1980), *Stallerhof* (1972) and *Ghost Train* (1972). I will base my comments partly on my production of *My Foot My Tutor*, which I directed in London in 1973 and on the production of *The Choice For Life*, broadcast as a radio play in 1973, revised for the stage by Kroetz and directed by Hartmut Baum in Munich in 1980. Like *My Foot My Tutor*, *Stallerhof* and *Ghost Train* are set in primitive rural circumstances and consist of short elliptical scenes; they share an attention to minute ordinary detail. The attitudes towards 'language' and the basic sets of relationships in Handke's mime play and Kroetz's dialect pieces about semi-articulate people, *Stallerhof* and *Ghost Train*, have similarities and in each case are typical of the authors' work.

Before the first production of *My Foot My Tutor* in 1969 Peter Handke had already achieved a reputation in the theatre with his short *Sprechstücke* – 'speaking plays' – and the full length *Kaspar*. As the generic term 'speaking play' implies, language itself was the chief substance *and* subject of Handke's first stage works. He eliminated plot, character and environment and in their place created linguistic constructs through which he could explore the sign systems unique to the theatre. *Offending The Audience*, typically, is an aggressively entertaining argument with the conventional theatre. Four figures assault the audience with a barrage of utterances about the act of going to the theatre, of making theatre, of the history of theatre – in other words, about the entire existential and historical context within which the four performers together with their audience find themselves. The play's action is its sentences, which are first stripped of meaning then reconstructed with meaning as the piece proceeds. Handke's suggestion to actors about using chants, rock rhythms and other formalized patterns of uttering sentences only take the analysis of performed language one step further, from the areas of 'pure' sentences to the area of 'speech acts'. With *Kaspar*, Handke continued in the linguistic mode, demonstrating the relationship between language and the individual consciousness by means of a single character and an unseen set of speech 'prompters' who inundate him with sentences, which he gradually seems to internalize.

Handke's attitude toward the phenomenon of language is no less paradoxical than it is familiar: he recognizes the strictures imposed by rules which govern its use, and by the systematic social and historical use of language forms to inhibit thought, and worse, to enslave. T. W. Adorno's famous remark on the German culture and language after the Third Reich is no less important, it would seem to Handke, than it was to an older generation of German language writers: 'to write a poem after Auschwitz is barbaric.' The German language itself had been debased. But Handke of course is a poet, and to him the freedom which each individual has, or ought to have, to 'tinker' with language, to create fresh worlds out of the imaginative rubble of civilization, is priceless. Implicit in all of his work is the idea that the liberation which 'free play' with language allows extends to human behaviour in general, and is the prerequisite for any other kind of liberation. As iconoclast, Handke assaults language as it is:

> For every one of my sentences the psychoanalyst applied a code which, however, was only part of another closed linguistic system; the job would be to de-systematize all closed linguistic systems; not to discover codes, but to decode all the ones which already exist.
>
> (*The Weight of the World*, pp. 61–62)

As poet, Handke sees the life of the imagination as primary: to nurture the free play of language and of spontaneity is to take a step towards personal, as he puts it, 'poetical power'.

When in 1969 he produced *My Foot My Tutor*, a play without a spoken word, Handke was not really breaking from his earlier language plays, only extending the limits of what he considered to be language. This short mime play extends the exploration of theatrical form and the languages of theatre, while continuing the meditation on the duality (stricture/free play) of language in the distinctive form of mime. *My Foot My Tutor* seems to be a very rigidly constructed play, all the movements of the two characters in a model master/slave relationship prescribed in a particular order, but Handke introduces details for

31

performance which subvert the apparent fixed structure. Often the achievement of harmony in life, Handke claims, is the result of pure chance – a wrinkle of consciousness, a happy coincidence of elements in experience and thought. In the theatre, as the surrealists before him noted, it is often this very chance factor which brings the art form to life and gives it its distinctive quality.

The title *My Foot My Tutor* derives from the late 'fantastic' theatre of Shakespeare, *The Tempest*, Act I, scene 2, in which Prospero, surprised by his daughter's rebuke at his having frozen Ferdinand in his tracks with a wave of the magic wand, asks her if the order of the world is to be turned upside down, if the foot is now to rule the head: 'What, I say, my foot my tutor?' The standard German translation for the line, '*Das Mündel will Vormund sein*' (the ward wants to be warden), is Handke's actual title, and explicitly denotes a theme one frequently encounters in his work: the nature of subservient relationships. In a radio interview Handke explained that the play 'mirrors power relationships and shows that control is also practical without words'. But thematic substance of this kind, as usual in Handke, is not necessarily the dominant element in the piece, and is inseparable from the author's active investigation of the theatre's formal means. In *My Foot My Tutor* Handke matter of factly debunks the sort of theatre which attempts to depict a reality in verifiable naturalistic terms: 'In the background of the stage we see, as the stage background, the façade of a farmhouse. The stage is not deep'. Handke's manner of describing the stage and the actions on it, forces the director and performers to make certain judgments about the nature of theatre art. By extension, the audience is forced to do the same. Working on the script, one becomes aware of the interpenetration of thematic material and formal means. Ideas cannot be abstracted from their enactment.

Perception in the theatre is a primary idea in the play. When Handke writes, 'In front of the farmhouse we see a peculiar, longish object and ask ourselves what it might represent' he is referring to the naturalistic theatre's habit of representing things, and to a conventional audience's inclination to want to decipher the representation. In the course of the play, Handke refers obliquely to some of the more blatant examples of representation and deciphering, typically derived from the popular mass 'dramatic' form, movies. While the warden clips his toenails, the ward responds by rushing to the wall calendar and tearing away, page by page, all of the leaves until only the cardboard backing remains: TIME PASSING. But Handke's concern with the workings of theatrical form necessarily brings him to consider on its own terms this essential feature of performance: time passing. Later in the play he will write: 'Some time passes, it has already passed.' The quotation of 'calendar leaves falling' debunks symbolic usages on stage, but Handke also draws one's attention to the actuality of time transpiring on stage, the time common to audience and performers. After the calendar business, the warden places the end of a rubber hose into the kettle, leaves the stage to turn on the water, returns and places the kettle on the hotplate. Then he drags the 'very long' hose on stage. Handke comments: 'Nothing funny happens.' That is, do not strain for comedy: if it is perceived as comical that's another matter.

> Quietly, contemplating each other, the two figures squat
> on stage.
> Gradually we begin to hear the water simmering in the
> kettle.

The noises we hear are those that are produced when
water is heated.

The actions performed are common enough, and
ordinarily denote certain relationships: one man clips his
nails, another fetches the parings; one man indicates 'hot
beverage', another man grinds the coffee. The basis of
much naturalistic effect in drama is in similar everyday
procedures. But for Handke, the details are important for
their aesthetic, not their descriptive, dimension. When the
stopper is 'probably blown off the kettle' a tension is
released (or isn't if it doesn't), but the tension is concrete,
derived from the (boringly) long wait for the water to boil,
and the joke has a proverbial basis, having to do with
'watched pots'. Felt time is what Handke is after. In the
second part of *They Are Dying Out* for the same purpose
he calls for a device reminiscent of late fifties American
'happenings': a block of ice is prominently displayed under
the lights, to melt in the time it takes for ice to melt under
theatre lights.

Musical accompaniment in *My Foot My Tutor* also has a
double purpose: serving a thematic idea in the play and
indicating another essential aspect of theatricality. Handke
specifies a piece of music, explains that it is to be played
over and over, occasionally refers to it in the text, and by
the very nature of the music chosen, allows the particular
flow of the theatrical event to be governed by the random
congruences of actions and chords. The Country Joe and
the Fish guitar piece Handke calls for, *Colors for Susan*,
has a dreamy and monotonous quality to it, very much in a
late sixties mode: Doors and Jefferson Airplane also come
to mind.

Before the music starts, at the beginning of the play, we
see the ward eating an apple, followed by the entrance of

the warden with a larger fruity sphere of his own, a pumpkin. The hat-bearing, pumpkin-toting, tattoo-decorated warden, by his very presence, it seems, forces the hatless, tattooless apple-eater into motionlessness. An 'ocular assault' has taken place.[1] The set changes, and the mysterious music sets in. As with the calendar leaves, the music denotes a cliché from popular dramatic form; it could be the ominous score for a 'B' thriller in the movies. Handke also calls for heavy unidentifiable breathing to be piped in, here and towards the end of the play, quoting an Italian detective film with Stewart Granger, *The Chief Sends His Best Man*, to help (!) the director or reader.

Handke describes the music as follows:

While it is gradually becoming completely dark, we hear music, a succession of chords piped in very much at random, with the pauses between them varying in length. Occasionally several chords follow each other in quick succession . . . . The piece only lasts five minutes and fifty seconds, so it's repeated over and over during the course of events, except for the very end of the tune, which is reserved for the end of the events.

Just as the invocation of time in the theatre through hackneyed symbols (calendar leaves) has its serious counterpart in the fact of water boiling and actual time passing, so the use of the 'B' movie reference to 'atmosphere' and 'tension' through the music has its serious side in the way the chords potentially effect the flow of movement.

At one point, he writes 'Now the music becomes nearly inaudible, just as the main theme may disappear almost entirely during certain sections of a film.' He signals changes in volume and the relative distinctness of sound in several places, but chooses not to score it exactly, in the way he had with sounds in his radio pieces. The randomness of the chords as they exist in the Country Joe music and as they accompany the mimed actions of the performers is an important element in itself.

One moment in which Handke draws attention to the chords gives an idea of his intention. The ward and warden have faced off for a sequence of actions: the warden reads a newspaper, folded to one page; the ward then produces a tiny book from his pocket and reads it; the warden folds his paper in half. While the ward draws with a pencil in the little book, then on his hand and arms, ('What he draws doesn't necessarily have to resemble the warden's tattoo'), the warden proceeds from folding to crumpling the paper. The warden then stares at the ward, crumpled paper in his hand. The ward pushes the pencil into his arm, then 'quickly pulls his hand away and places it, slowly, on the lower part of the arm with the drawing on it'. The crumpled paper is released, and as it 'slowly expands', Handke comments: 'The music, noticeably louder now, is pleasant.' The comment, like others about 'nothing funny' happening here, is typical of Handke's playful sense of the theatre's possibilities, and subtle traps. Of course he cannot know whether the same monotonous chords are pleasant or not at this moment to any given audience; nor can the performers easily express such a mood, half masked as they are. The comment is whimsical, but also underscores pure chance as an active stage element. In their 1975 production of the play, the Freies Theater München decided to use the music only at the beginning and the end of the production. In their very intimate theatre space, according to director George Froscher, they chose to allow sounds like crumpling paper to 'speak for themselves'.

Kroetz and Handke: A Comparison

In *Kaspar* (1968) the main figure learns piecemeal about the phenomena in his environment. His look-alike figures take a ball and demonstrate it rolling, or 'refusing' to roll, across a stage. The piped-in words of the prompters announce: 'Movement.' Elsewhere an intractable closet door 'moves of its own accord.' At the equivalent moment in *My Foot My Tutor*, the chords strike, quickly or not, softly or not, at one level of volume or another, and the paper ball unfolds itself. The moment is evocative, but its mood or meaning is imponderable beyond the precise moment at which it occurs. In the course of the performance of *My Foot My Tutor* the stroke of a guitar chord accompanying a prescribed movement or gesture creates a quality unique to that particular moment. All of the apparently rigid prescribed movements transcend their choreography, as it were, by being subject to the random stroke of a guitar. Handke highlights the unfixable fixed form of rehearsed theatre, its 'liveness', by the choice of Country Joe and the Fish's *Colors for Susan*, and the broad hints that the interplay of sound and action should not be too strictly arranged. This aspect of the play, and its effect on the flow of movement of the performers, as well as audience response, becomes clear in repeated performances of the play. Any given stage occurrence, as trivial as sitting down or standing up, or as ominous as blood dripping from one figure's nose while the other watches motionless, acquires a distinctive tone depending on the order and intensity of the chords in the music.

The 'particular moment' is extremely important for Handke. In his 1977 journal (*The Weight of the World*) he describes the sad spectacle of Alexander Solzhenitsyn who, having learned how to perform on Western television, gives the impression of fraud even though he is saying things which may be true and which he believes. He has

37

become someone using mere 'forms to convince' because at the *moment* he speaks he does not feel what he is saying and does not make the effort at that moment to feel what he is saying. Handke's art attempts to prepare the ground for spontaneous moments, 'moments of true feeling', to quote the title of one of his novels.

What at first appears to be just another amusing stab at naturalist theatre, and a not so minor nightmare for directors, the presence of a live cat on stage, is a consistent extension of the idea of spontaneity in Handke's use of music.

On the chopping block, next to the large piece of wood with the hatchet sticking in it, we notice a cat: while the curtain opens, the cat probably raises its head and subsequently does what it usually does, so that we recognize: the cat represents what it does. The cat does what it does. If it should decide to leave the stage, no one should stop it from doing so.

The cat suddenly slinks out of the house. . . .
The cat does what it does.

The choice of an eminently unrehearsable domestic animal as one of the 'actors' guarantees spontaneity. Once the cat is seen on stage, freely moving or remaining still, the entire piece is affected by its presence or its conspicuous absence. To eliminate the cat altogether, as was done at the premiere production, seems to be a mistake, as does the substitution of another animal, a rooster, say, as was used in a touring Munich production in 1971.

In the production I directed a curious moment occurred because of the cat during one performance, in a section of the play shortly after the kettle scene described above. After the warden has gone off stage to fetch a frying pan which contains fuming incense, he enters with it in one hand and a piece of chalk in the other, with which he inscribes the traditional year's end 'K + M + B' (the initials of the three wise men) on the door. While he is doing so, the ward throws light missiles at him, which stick to his back. They are burs. The warden takes a bullwhip from the wall, turns, 'as though accidentally, not quickly; at the same time, the ward throws a bur, which hits the warden's chest (or not). The warden is standing there by himself; the ward throws the remaining burs at the warden.' The stage 'becomes dark once again, and the music . . . continues.'

It was in the next scene that the cat was to appear. The stage is peaceful, yet filled with the afterglow of the muted violence of the previous actions:

> The two figures are sitting on the stage, which is bright again; they are sitting at the table, each one by himself.
> They are sitting, each one by himself.
> They are sitting, each one by himself.
> They are sitting, each one by himself.
> They are sitting, each one by himself.
> They are sitting, each one by himself.
> All at once we notice there is blood running from the ward's nose.
> The blood trickles out of his nose, across his mouth, over his chin, out of his nose . . .
> The warden is sitting there by himself, the ward doesn't budge from the spot, doesn't budge from the spot . . .
> Gradually it becomes dark again on the stage.

As the two figures sat there during one performance, and the ward turned his head slightly downstage to reveal the dripping blood, the cat returned to the stage for the first time since the opening moments of the play, and climbed onto the table. It watched, while the audience watched, the blood trickle from the ward's nose. Then it left the stage for the night. After the performance someone asked how the cat had been trained. It had not.

That was the point. The cat's behaviour is not really predictable, even if one strives to limit the range of possibilities, say, with mild starvation and tunafish placed on a tree trunk the instant before the first curtain. What transpires on stage has a chance element, which is highlighted by the presence (and absence) of the cat. When the Freies Theater München produced *My Foot My Tutor* in 1975 their cat had a habit of settling into the audience in the round, choosing a comfortable lap to perch in. It was a particularly independent cat, they explained, allowed to wander freely during the day and picked up for the show at night. During the run of the show it was struck by a car and killed. They decided to continue the run without a cat. Though the audiences had no way of knowing this, that too was the point, one supposes, with a vengeance. The ominousness of a mute confrontation and the sudden appearance of blood dripping from a nostril, is redoubled (or negated: giggling could easily break out) by the reappearance of an unpredictable animal. The effect cannot be calculated. And so it is in much of Handke's theatre work, where the form is open and a spirit of inventiveness and experimentation prevails.

The last time the two figures are on stage together in *My Foot My Tutor*, the warden undrapes the mysterious object we saw at the start of the play to reveal it as a beet-cutting machine. The warden easily lops off the top of a

large Bavarian beet, about the size of a head, then the ward
sets to trying the same with intermittent success. The cat
corralled if possible during the blackout, comes through
the cat-flap in the door to the exterior scene, and 'does
what it does'. While the barefoot warden walks about the
stage the ward keeps trying to work the machine.

> . . . then – it is already quite dark (is the warden
> standing by the machine?) – finally once more, and now
> – we can't bear watching it anymore – once again, and
> we don't hear the sound of anything falling on the floor;
> thereupon it is quiet onstage, for quite some time.

Nothing explicit here, with two antagonists and a cat in a
protracted chopping scene; but when the piped-in sound
('a death rattle?', Handke asks) reaches a crescendo 'too
large for the house', then dies down, the lights come up
and we see only a bare bright stage. Then a figure appears:
it is the ward. He no longer wears his overalls, Handke tells
us, and he carries the long rubber hose wound about the
upper part of his body, suggesting perhaps a snake, an
image which is found elsewhere in Handke's fiction and
plays. The last moment of *They Are Dying Out* calls for
snakes to swarm about the stage floor. The ward's actions
are strange distorted echoes of the warden's in a previous
scene. He takes the hose and with it fills a larger receptacle,
a tub, just as the warden had earlier filled a kettle. The idea
of chance and free play in the theatrical form, a *jeu
d'esprit* and desire for momentary escape from binding
structures relates here to social reality. The ward too,
wants to be free, as the literal German title, *The Ward
Wants to Be The Warden*, clearly states. The irony of the
title is that freedom implies an endless chain of wards and
wardens. In a production of the play the year after it

premiered this idea formed the basis of the approach to the piece: it was presented as a struggle for liberation from bondage. One would not need to stress such an interpretation throughout, to see it as a possibility in the waning moments of the play. Handke's play in 1969, in the minimalist mode, opposes an archetypal tyranny, of one master and one slave, while it celebrates the free play of elements in the theatre. Handke told Kroetz in a television interview that 'The greatest effort in writing is to save the pure chance aspects of life.' *My Foot My Tutor*, while radically different from the large scale documentary pieces of the early sixties by Hochhuth, Weiss and others which opposed specific tyrannies, shares a desire to unfetter the individual.

In a programme note to the first production of *My Foot My Tutor* in 1969, Handke gives an example of a tiny 'sensation' – in 1966 in Bayreuth before a performance of Wagner's *Tristan* he put a coin in a parking meter for the first time in his life. The trivial activity of putting the coin in the meter is given precedence over the great work of art, *Tristan*, because the novel sensation was of greater personal importance to him at that time. A feature of Handke's theatre is the attention paid to tiny detail, not as in the naturalist mode with the intent of putting together a composite picture of reality, but rather with the purpose of discovering its mystery, sometimes simply to celebrate it, sometimes to rebel against it. The fact of pouring water and sand or preparing coffee or cutting toenails is accepted for what it is, with no symbolism intended. The extension of the theme of presenting the bare facts of subservient relations, and their possible resolution, however vaguely suggested, achieves its power from the limits of the author's intentions.

While Handke abjures blueprints for the future,

revolutionary proclamations and programmatic all-encompassing systems, his insight into the miniscule details of the facts of power relations and the scope of alienation, is remarkably accurate, and moving. 'You're too good for us to let you go', Kroetz commented to him in their television debate.

Handke's linguistic analysis has led critics to relate his work to the analytical linguistic philosophy of the Austrian Ludwig Wittgenstein. There is a spirit in Handke's early plays which seems to be searching for 'simple propositions', well knowing they are not to be found. In *My Foot My Tutor* and other Handke works the later thoughts of Wittgenstein seem also to apply. The later Wittgenstein approached the task of philosophy more with the eye of an artist than that of an analyst. He published hardly a thing, but uttered cryptic remarks about the whole area of experience beyond logic and language, felt to be there, as in dreams, though never tangible nor precisely knowable. The subjectivity in Handke's writing is relentlessly critical: he himself, his own thoughts are typical models for the thoughts of his generation.

Whereas Handke underscores the contingency of theatricality as such in *My Foot My Tutor* by his use of a cat and random chords on the guitar, Kroetz's *The Choice For Life* in 1980 based its particular aesthetic on another sort of theatrical contingency. As a public performance art theatre can interact with the society in which it occurs in a unique manner. Hartmut Baum, director of the production at the Munich Theater Rechts der Isar, true to the spirit of Kroetz's work, began the election-eve preview with a long prelude during which the father of the family in Kroetz's three person play sat alone in an easy chair watching a televised debate (taped several days before) between the principal spokesmen for the major parties involved in the

1980 federal election: Helmut Schmidt (Social Democratic Party); Franz Josef Strauss (Christian Social Union); Helmut Kohl (Christian Democratic Union); Hans Dietrich Genscher (Free Democratic Party). Schmidt and Strauss were the representatives of the SPD/FDP, and CSU/CDU coalitions respectively, in the elections. On opening night instead of the taped debate which the majority of the audience would already have seen, the television the father in the play watched had the live broadcast of the election results, larded with the usual commentary.

The play deals with a young man's decision that he would rather not work for the armaments industry, regardless of pay and prestige, because someone sometime has to choose to resist escalating preparations for war. The two other characters in the play, his lower middle class mother and father, try to talk him out of his decision: why did we pay for engineering school?; someone has to work for our security; what will the neighbours say? It turns out the father has a vivid memory as one of the wallpaperers who had the dubious privilege of finishing the interior of Dachau's headquarters. His wife reminds him how upset he was at the time by what he had seen. In the end, typical of one strain in Kroetz's later work, the mother and father make an enlightened choice to support their son's decision.

The *Wahl* in Kroetz's title, *Die Wahl fürs Leben* typically for his work, is a pun, meaning either choice or election. The 1980 election context, and the running discussion on the television in the background, provided a special immediacy to the play. With a taped debate it was possible to highlight particularly significant juxtapositions in the play's dialogue and in the words of important political figures, though in the opening night production this was left more to chance in the assumption that the TV debate and the stage dialogue would intersect at some point. When the son, Karli, argues against taking the job with a large firm whose main source of income is defence contracts, the mother explains that his job would be 'in the interest of security'. At this moment in Baum's production one heard CDU representative Kohl on the TV, claiming with unintentional irony that the rightist parties had an interest in preserving peace too, with the words: 'They are our common dead.' This political reality, brought into the theatre in a country with a war experience as brutally specific as Germany's, silenced the audience. Kroetz, an active director and actor as well as playwright, remains attuned to the issues of the moment and to the manner in which they can most effectively be made into theatre. The political figures speaking for themselves on television are a literal fulfilment of Kroetz's desire to extend the types of characters in his plays: 'When I want to say something about power, I must bring the powerful to speak.' The archetypal struggle for power in *My Foot My Tutor* has its very concrete parallel in Kroetz's play.

The visual presence in *The Choice For Life* of the political figures from the 'world theatre', prominently displayed on a colour TV in the all white box-like room of Baum's 1980 production, reinforces the kind of contingency which Kroetz finds important to his theatre work. 'The total context is what you must consider', Kroetz told me, 'when thinking of the work we realists are engaged in.' In the case of *The Choice For Life* this context, besides the larger historical one of a divided Germany which has experienced the two world wars, would include the facts of the political situation in 1980. Less than a fortnight before the production of Kroetz's play, the chief spokesman for the CDU/CSU, Franz Josef

Strauss had paraded through Munich amidst the pomp of the traditional Oktoberfest processional; a week after that a right-wing extremist from the 'Wehrsportgruppe Hoffmann' had blown himself and a few dozen others to kingdom come at the Oktoberfest main gate; an alternate procession had passed through Munich the night before Strauss, the piece of street theatre in which Hanne Hiob Brecht was involved. On small stages in Munich any number of cabaret performers could also be seen performing satirical sketches caricaturing the primary antagonists in the election, which the audience for *The Choice For Life* saw on the stage television. This example of a Kroetz play at a specific historical moment is a special case, but represents one important tendency in Kroetz's work.

When in 1977 Kroetz and Handke talked on television about their work Handke expressed his feelings that fleeting 'harmonies' in life, political and personal, occur only by chance. Not that he wants it that way, but that is the way it happens to be. In *My Foot My Tutor* the idea seems to be part of his aesthetic. The illusion of 'chance' as a governing factor in the real world, according to Kroetz, plays into the hands of those in a capitalist society who are in control. In *The Choice For Life* he uses a 'live' TV show as part of a total context to point out connections between the lives of ordinary people and the dealings of the powerful: a random selection as it were.

Up to about the time of his affiliation with the German Communist Party in 1972, Kroetz's work was in the tradition of descriptive naturalism, which accurately depicted particular milieus without actively commenting on them. With success and the opportunity, especially in radio and television, to reach greater numbers of people, he concerned himself increasingly with the specific

46

problems of 'average citizens'. Though some of his work addresses specific German issues and is therefore unlikely to translate well, most of the plays, *The Choice For Life* being a good example, do have a wider applicability.

Stallerhof and *Ghost Train* were written and produced at a time when Kroetz's political intentions were not yet so definitely articulated, but the basic assumptions of naturalism govern their form, distinguishing them from Handke's work. They possess the distinctive qualities of Kroetz's best dramatic work. The two plays tell the story of a physically and mentally handicapped farm girl in her teens, Beppi, who has a child by an older worker near retirement age, Sepp, with whom she and the baby eventually set up house. Beppi and Sepp are common enough Bavarian diminutive names, but they also possess the root of the pejorative nickname or insult, 'Depp', which means 'goof' or 'idiot'. The three of them survive more or less harmoniously on piece-work done at home until Sepp dies of pneumonia. Rather than let the authorities, tipped off by her parents, claim the child, Beppi affectionately smothers it and places the body on a 'ghost train' in an amusement park 'spook house'. *Stallerhof* ends up with Beppi crying out in labour with child; *Ghost Train* ends with her in jail, asking her mother and father if she can have her pet hamster, Konrad.

In Handke's *My Foot My Tutor* the environment is of minimal importance, valued mainly for its part in an experimental aesthetic. The warden wears a blue and white checked shirt, a kind of Bavarian flag, as an amusing note on 'ruralness', not as a way of placing him in a region. For Kroetz, who has said his early plays (and one imagines many of the later ones) were the result of direct experience with particular people in specific environments, the rural setting has a naturalistic function: this is the feel of things

47

in certain depressed rural areas. Handke's interest in the workings and limits of language in general leads him to an experiment in *My Foot My Tutor* with pure gesture in an archetypal relationship. His comments elsewhere make it clear that Handke is aware that the patterns embedded in the functioning 'language' of a culture can be socially repressive. This is one of the ruling ideas in *Kaspar*, treated in the abstract, and a theme of *My Foot My Tutor*. Kroetz presents the theme realistically.

Patterns of formula speech are found in most of Kroetz's plays, serving several different functions. In Act II, scene 1 of *Ghost Train* Sepp and Beppi are together in their rented room:

SEPP: You can't defend yourself if you're the weaker one.
BEPPI: Nothing ventured nothing gained!
SEPP: (*looks at her*) You got that from me, right!
BEPPI: (*nods*)
SEPP: That's a proverb, that's all.
BEPPI: Nothing ventured nothing gained!
SEPP: (*smiling*) God helps those who help themselves!

In the next scene Beppi's mother and father discuss their daughter's departure:

STALLER: They're gone anyway.
STALLERIN: Just like we wanted.
STALLER: Because I was asked if that's what I wanted.
STALLERIN: God helps those who help themselves.
STALLER: That's a proverb, that's all.
STALLERIN: But it's true.

Kroetz remarked on several occasions that he is interested in the gap between what people may feel or think and what they are capable of articulating. The early plays, including *Stallerhof* and *Ghost Train*, deal with people more or less on the fringes of society, where the inadequacies of speech are most acute. While the use of proverbs and other types of formula speech are often in grotesque discord with the realities of his characters' situations ('God helps those who help themselves' is more than a little ironic coming from a crippled retarded teenage mother living in *concubinage* with an over-the-hill lover soon to die of pneumonia), and often signal the dead end of personal expression and of any hope of working out one's problems through conversation, it can also serve a purpose beyond the mere words uttered. In the first scene quoted above Sepp has taught Beppi something, and although it is a cliché, the real communication is in the act of teaching. For the parents in the later scene the same cliché functions normally, and communication stops.

The numerous pauses in these plays, surrounding simple, sometimes brute actions, represent an interesting analogue to the silent 'communication' in *My Foot My Tutor*. A very deep mute violence is in the air. In *Stallerhof* the actions are at first of this sort:

[*at the funfair*]
(*They go behind a tent or away from the crowd.*) SEPP: Here, wipe yourself with these leaves. (*She cleans herself; diarrhoea runs down her legs.*) Here let me. (*He cleans her up.*) SEPP: You shit your pants. Take off your pants, you can't run around like that. (*Beppi cleans herself with his help.*) Wipe yourself with this – Here let me. (*He takes his handkerchief and wipes her with it.*) It's alright again. (*pause*) Come here. (*He takes her and deflowers her.*)

But eventually they display mutual tenderness, still largely mute, while they are simply at work together, or after they make love. The communication of feeling transcends the limits of their vocabulary. There is a danger that this sort of relationship on stage could descend into sheer pathos or sentimentality, but Kroetz's matter of fact way of presenting it and its very sparseness militates against that. Working with the famous actress Therese Giehse on his play *Future Prospects* about an old woman preparing to enter an old folks' home, Kroetz has noted that this problem existed in some of his work and how Giehse's acting itself saved his play from sentimentality.

When Handke criticized Kroetz's work he said that this technique of identification and emotional arousal had become a *perpetuum mobile* in all of Kroetz's plays, a point which Kroetz himself implicitly accepts in that he has consciously experimented with ways of avoiding it. The formula speech which represents a blockage of thought for her parents has become a vehicle for communication, despite the words, for Beppi. Brute actions – rape, emotional exploitation – transform themselves into something else in the course of the plays, though the outcome is far from utopian. The last mute tender act of 'love' in *Ghost Train* is infanticide.

In Kroetz's plays the sets of relationships are identifiable: parents/daughter; employer/employee; man/woman. Beppi gradually grows more articulate, in a pattern familiar in the realist tradition. Like Kaspar, she defends herself with a sentence, though her rehearsed sentence ironically threatens suicide if her parents take away her child. The first person singular is her assertion of independence.

STALLERIN: Papa's right. We mean well if you could only understand.

BEPPI: I

STALLERIN: But we're not talking about you. You're still young.

Beppi, typically for Kroetz, becomes a free person through the social and biological facts of mutual dependency, with the baby, and with Sepp.

In the end her new freedom and articulacy are useless, however, as she destroys the child (and herself, symbolically) in response to the missive from the authorities, which is an example of another kind of oppressive language:

Dear Mr. Mrs. Miss Staller. In accordance with the social worker's decision of 30.3 1972 the temporary committal of your son daughter George Staller born on 10.1 1971. . . .

Beppi's meticulous preparation of her son's cardboard carrying case/coffin, complete with 'breathing holes', like her mother's very orderly preparation for Beppi's departure in an earlier scene, if given its full weight in performance, can be chilling because of its simplicity. The time it takes to perform these actions on stage should be the time they would take in real life, Kroetz insists. In performance they go on and on, rather like Handke's boiling water, but for a different effect and purpose.

The entire action of Kroetz's silent one woman piece, *Request Concert* which premiered in 1971, consists of the banal activities of an ordinary working woman at the end of a day, and of a life – after cleaning up and preparing for bed, she turns out the light. Then, as if in an afterthought, she switches it on and spreads pills before her in orderly fashion and proceeds to swallow them. This choice for death in the early seventies had become a choice for life in 1980.

4
Handke: Short Pieces and 'Kaspar'

Handke once disparagingly described the conventional theatre as 'geometrically this right angled relationship, in which people on the stage speak to one another, while others look at them'. His first plays challenge that relationship. *Offending The Audience* (1966), in a tradition stemming at least from the Dadaist movement, has performers directing their gaze squarely at the audience. 'We form a unit,' they assert at the beginning of the script, then descend to provocative audience abuse: 'You were born actors. Play acting was in your blood, you butchers, you buggers, you bullshitters, you bullies, you rabbits, you fuck-offs, you farts.' Implicitly the point seems to have been to push some members of the audience to the limits of endurance, to break down the fourth wall, or at least to chip away at the brickwork. Handke responded to what he considered overly jaunty early productions and to the occasional rowdy audience reaction by withdrawing performance rights for *Offending The Audience* and explaining in his published collected plays

(1972) that his real intention was to encourage audiences to meditate on the ideas of 'language' and 'theatre'. Though his tongue was no doubt tucked into his cheek for the remark on 'meditation' in the theatre, one can understand Handke's reluctance to allow his play to be permanently identified with a particular (late sixties) form of aggressiveness toward audiences.

When asked his feelings in 1975 about his early work, Handke further claimed that he found two of the plays, *Prophecy* (1966) and *Calling for Help* (1967), too slick and overly formalistic, and thought his whole corpus would be better off if they could be removed. Both of these 'speaking plays' continue the exploration of the limits of language and performance, however, and are interesting in the development of the playwright. There are four speakers in *Prophecy*, designated 'A, B, C, D', who utter two hundred and eight tautological statements in combinations of voices. What Handke hoped to achieve was 'an acoustic field as compact as possible, which in turn produces the most penetrating acoustic irritation'. The fact of live performance adds resonance to the idea of metaphor: a stage is a place where men and women normally play men and women, a self-referring metaphor in itself, and unique to theatre. Concluding the play are the lines: 'D: The skin will be skin-deep; C: The blood thirsty will be bloodthirsty; B: The threads will be threadbare; A: The stone will be stone hard.' The last line is pronounced by all four: 'Every day will be like every other.' That depressing conclusion is modified by the fact that in the art of live drama, as Handke describes the 'open' form, not every performance will be like the last.

In *Calling For Help* an unspecified number of speakers (minimum two) utter single sentences, then words, with increasing vigour for approximately fifteen minutes. Each utterance elicits a simple 'NO' from another speaker or group of speakers. At the end of the piece the question 'help?' is asked, and 'pure joy reigns among the speakers'. Handke's preface explains that 'The speakers' objective is to show the way to the sought-after word HELP, a way that leads across many sentences and words . . . on their way to the word help, the speakers repeatedly approach the proximate meaning or only the acoustic proximity of the sought-after word: the respective NO-response that greets each attempt also changes according to the degree of proximity . . .'

A note on performance for the premiere of *Self-Accusation* (1966), also a 'grammatical' play, specified two speakers, a man and a woman, voices attuned to each other, who are to use microphones and loudspeakers. In the 1972 edition Handke suggested a 'new performance possibility'; that it be done by one speaker, without the help of microphone and with no rhythmic formalization. The play consists of statements by an 'I' figure, which Handke is at pains to keep impersonal: the grammatical 'I' and not the subjective referent is meant. 'Because the self-accusation is not that of a definite being', Handke writes, 'at each performance something new happens, the self-accusation is always that of those just then present. . .'.

Self-Accusation begins with the momentous line, 'I came into the world', and winds down on a speculation which echoes both Handke's religious background and the formal suggestion for delivery of the piece – as in a confessional:

I did not regard the demands of reason for immortality as proof of life after death. I did not regard my nausea as the thought of the future as proof of my non-existence after death.

But in Handke's humorous manner, statements like the above are no more significant than others about 'cleaning the sidewalk' or 'keeping one's eyes open during sexual intercourse'.

Quodlibet (1970) leaves more to the imaginations of directors and performers than do any of Handke's other short pieces. He explains that the 'director and actor must discover the details through experimentation. It would be nonsense in this connection if the play didn't remain "open".' Handke's use of costumed 'characters' from the WORLD THEATRE, politicians, bishops, generals, and his emphasis on movement, also set it apart from the other *Sprechstücke*. Although a central motif is still the language-complex, this piece extends the experiment to include physical movement.

A structural feature of *Quodlibet*, which Handke was at pains to clarify in answer to a rather dismissive *Theater heute* review of the play, was the fact that the phases of the play 'don't develop in linear order, but are mixed into one another, sometimes even occurring at the same time'. The phases referred to are the 'speech figures' which constitute the bulk of the written text, and the corresponding visual and kinetic elements. Among the 'speech figures' are: 'misunderstandings, allusions, stories, quotations, opinion and counter-opinion, joke-telling, stories as EXAMPLES for something, whereby the given listener himself provides another EXAMPLE . . . monologues, which expect only confirming silence as an answer, monologues which actually 'just slip out' and which aren't meant to be heard by anyone, *etc.*'. These and other configurations of 'talking activities' determine the 'characters', as it were, not the other way around. And it is the job of 'actors and director to collaborate in investigating which moving image or static image is created out of a specific speech situation in reality'. Through the 'theatrical ornaments' so produced, one gains insight into such 'ornaments' in reality. Above all, Handke stresses, the piece 'must play to the audience in one single living movement'. In conversation about *Quodlibet* and *The Ride Across Lake Constance*, for which the former was a prelude, Handke volunteered a fondness for Chekhov's theatre, rather than, as the interviewer had proposed, Ionesco's. In some respects, *Quodlibet* is like an abstraction of all those half-heard and hardly understood scraps of small talk which form the basis of Chekhov's theatre: a tapestry of Chekhovian murmur. Handke removes the 'history' and 'psychology' of his characters, and patterns of talk remain. As an experimental piece of theatre, *Quodlibet* extends the field of interest to those parts of plays in performance when, for whatever reason, the attention strays and 'not everything is taken in'. The parallel social reality is obvious.

The literal 'Quodlibet' of the title refers not just to the performers' liberty to use the script as a basis for improvisation to create the 'single living movement' of speech and movement figures, but to the audience's role in making the half-heard, overheard, 'just glimpsed in passing' action of the performers into a construct of its own liking. If an audience member wants a construct, as he usually gets in the theatre, or even wants to make sense of isolated bits, he will have to do the work on his own. There is no 'meaning' intended. Handke's point seems to be that this is what people do all the time anyway: perceived reality as a Rorschach test. In the novel, *The Goalie's Anxiety at the Penalty Kick*, published the same year as the premiere of *Quodlibet*, the central figure, Bloch, has an encounter which is analogous to what an audience might experience at a performance of the play. Two policemen speak to

Bloch but 'seem to mean something entirely different' by their usual remarks:

> . . . at least they purposely mispronounced phrases like 'got to remember' and 'take off' as 'goats you remember' and 'take-off' and, just as purposely, let their tongues slide over others, saying 'whitewash?' instead of 'why watch?' and 'closed, or' instead of 'close door.'

Handke explicitly states that he doesn't want to give the audience of *Quodlibet* time to reflect in the manner Bloch does here, but the sense of his text indicates that the audience must, in the course of the performance, catch itself in the process of mistaking one phrase for another, or ascribing a false sense to a set of gestures. To begin with, the audience is meant to hear and understand certain words and sentences, including 'irrelevant and meaningless' ones like 'Do you understand?'. Then come the ones the audience only 'thinks it understands' because it is in the habit of doing so in the theatre:

> These are words and expressions which in the theatre act like bugle calls: political expressions, expressions relating to sex, the anal sphere, violence. Of course, the audience does not really hear the actual expressions but only similar ones; the latter are the signal for the former; the audience is bound to hear the right ones.

As with the 'insults' in *Offending The Audience*, here the words which are 'heard even when they are not there' are culturally determined. The German text contains a series of phrases related to *the* dominant subject in central European consciousness since World War II: typically, instead of hearing 'aus-schwitz' (sweat), an audience will hear 'Auschwitz'. In Michael Roloff's translation for Americans the 'no palms' will be decoded as 'napalm'. When Handke writes in the text, 'the *bomb* turns out to be *what a bomb this play was*, the *smashed brain on the stone* turns into *mashed potatoes alone, etc.*', he is implying that the performers should play in such a way as to lead the audience to recognize some of its 'errors'.

Handke covers himself in the event of interfering audience members by suggesting the actors use typical politicians' retorts to hecklers. Should someone come onto the stage, Handke has provided two bodyguards in the WORLD THEATRE cast who are gently to remove the person. 'To let the person remain on stage would only be a show of disdain.' There is an irony here in that *Quodlibet* seems to depend more on the old theatre's 'right angle' relationship between performers and audience, but the actual production history of Handke's other similar pieces led to the point where the author could expect disruptive interference from certain audiences. Here again he was forced to take this aspect of live theatre, into account: the aspect constituted by the history of Handke performances.

The printed lines in *Quodlibet* contain the familiar obsessions and jokes of Handke's other works, including satirical remarks about authority. Hence the WORLD THEATRE cast is only from the more comfortable or 'important' niches of society. The line 'All I had to do was "smile" at him and blood began pouring from his nose', in the series of 'wrong words instead of correct words' when both parties know the *real* word intended, evokes the striking image of power relationships from *My Foot My Tutor*. There is a corny story about a murder ('ice pick lodged in his head'), which ends in a very stagy croaking death rattle; a flash of flesh when a 'lady lifts her dress,

59

beneath which she is completely naked'; and a cornucopia of possibilities for improvisation. The particulars of actualization reside with the actors.

Handke's radio plays, with titles like *Sound of a Sound*, *Radio Play*, *Radio Play 2*, parallel his stage experiments in the way they explore the medium for which they were composed. Perhaps the most striking of the radio works is the 'voyage through consciousness', as Handke describes *Wind and Sea* (1970). Formally it resembles the stage experiment *Quodlibet* which appeared in the same year. *Quodlibet* sought to achieve a 'single flowing movement' of 'speech figures' and their visual equivalents which the audience glimpses in passing. *Wind and Sea* necessarily reduces the 'flowing movement' to sound, and of course eliminates the aspect of performance which relies on the presence of a live audience. No hecklers here. But the radio play, as all pieces written in that form, extends the work of the listener in constructing an inner imaginative landscape out of the arrangement of words and pure sound. A pioneer in the concept of the 'new arts', John Cage, had as much influence on the sixties boom of experimental radio pieces in Germany as did anyone. Testament to his continuing importance is the West German Rundfunk's (Köln) presentation in January of 1980 of his *Roaratorio – An Irish Circus about Finnegan's Wake*, in which, according to the brochure, 'the listener forms his own experiences'. Handke's pieces, normally less abstract than Cage's, present stimuli for the imagination, and let the listener's natural compulsion to construct a story do the rest.

Listening to Heinz Von Cramer's production of *Wind and Sea* (West German Rundfunk, Köln, 1971), one understands what Handke meant when he said he wanted to 'envelop' audiences with his short plays. The flow of sounds ranges from whispered children's voices to the roaring of the 'wind and sea'. Handke's script begins with the 'rather loud' voices of two children. No emotional tone is indicated for the voices, and Von Cramer chose to have his performers speak perfectly 'neutrally', disappointing normal expectations:

It surprises me to hear from you that your parents died last night.

The other child speaks also without emotion, describing a scene from the past: seeing the father approach, in sandals, holding a dogless leash and wearing a piece of folded white paper on his sunburned nose, an image from Handke's youth. Later the face will be 'fully burned', according to the child. In the course of the eleven minute tape one hears the sounds of adults uttering ever shorter phrases, as a child might overhear them from another room, the repeated message over a loudspeaker 'Attention, attention, Rennes Station is Closed', the sounds of wind and sea in different volumes, loud breathing. At the end all one hears is WIND AND SEA. In Germany, which has a prestigious award for radio theatre called the 'Radio Prize of the War Blind', it wouldn't be difficult to imagine the expected leap of the imagination in a context suggesting death, conflagration and general emergency to take the listener from the 'neutral' sounds of sea and wind to those of blanket bombing and fire storms. Von Cramer's production evokes these images. The play develops from the emotionless child's voice signalling the 'death of parents' at the start, to an environment of pure sound which doesn't communicate a fear and a sadness with words, but which produces it viscerally in the listener.

61

'Kaspar'

Kaspar (1968), his first full length play, is the most frequently produced of Handke's works and has attracted numerous important directors, including Peter Brook. Seven years after its premiere, Handke told an interviewer he would like to direct it himself some day, in a manner avoiding the usual means of the *'avant-garde'* – 'to show slowly and quietly how a figure is constructed, how this figure grows into something, and then returns to nothing. Without these loudspeakers, without these masks, *etc.*'[1] Handke saw two versions of Brook's production, the second of which transformed 'Handke's austere and verbal play' into 'a musical with very little dialogue (half the words went entirely), movement, dancing, songs . . .'. Brook described the final product as 'a fine version that could scoop in any audience', and claimed that Handke himself preferred this shortened and adapted *Kaspar* to the one which adhered more closely to the text.[2] Handke's running argument with the theatre, even his own, is a mark of his desire to keep things from becoming static, reduced to a fixed order. A central theme of *Kaspar* has to do with just that open imaginative capacity which defies stasis. He is concerned with what language, and by extension literature, can be made to do in a positive and negative sense.

In *A Sorrow Beyond Dreams* (1972), a 'life story' written after the suicide of his mother, Handke parenthetically muses on the problem of dealing with certain 'realities' in literature. One of the images (dreams perceived physically as worms) corresponds to a key image (black worms in the dark) in *Kaspar*:

'(In stories we often read that something or other is

"unnameable" or "indescribable"; ordinarily this strikes me as a cheap excuse. This story, however, is really about the nameless, about speechless moments of terror. It is about moments when the mind boggles with horror, states of fear so brief that speech always comes too late; about dream happenings so gruesome that the mind perceives them physically as worms. The blood curdles, the breath catches . . . in short, it is a record of states, not a well-rounded story with an anticipated, hence comforting, end.)'

The theatre at its most effective has the capability of inducing such states, unmediated, and uncannily in public. The audience finds itself at one point in the play, in the dark together with Kaspar himself, contemplating this impossible image of 'black worms in the dark'. In *Kaspar*, Handke continues his exploration of the facts of language and of theatre, of the tension between 'states of feeling' and the utterances which record them, and of the double capacity of language: on the one hand as a tool of a vaguely defined thought police who control the linguistic creation Kaspar, and who themselves are bound by the structures, grammatical and otherwise, which define any language; and on the other as the medium which allows one to create fictions 'out of nothing' and thereby to exercise a kind of personal freedom. The play turns on this ancient paradox.

The action of *Kaspar* is as follows. Two figures are dominant: Kaspar himself and an unseen set of prompters – 'three persons, say'. 'Over a good amplifying system' the disembodied voices of the Prompters 'speak a text that is not theirs' in the process first of bringing Kaspar to the good order of regular speech, and then of driving him quite mad by virtue of a physical assault with words. The principle of verbal saturation applies equally to the spectators, who must even suffer through the interval to the drone of piped-in text, such as: 'A screwdriver in the windpipe is appropriate remuneration for someone who never did anything but someone else's duty.' Kaspar enters the world of the theatre through an upstage curtain exactly like the main one downstage, suggesting an infinity of receding curtains. He is armed with one sentence, though it possesses no meaning for him: 'I want to be a person like somebody else was once.' After undergoing a protracted 'speech torture' which strips him of that sentence, he learns to use others and 'be rational'. By the end of the play, five 'somebody elses' like *him* in the form of exact look-alikes join Kaspar. All six wear masks of 'contentment', whereas Kaspar at the outset had worn a mask indicating 'astonishment and confusion'. The last moments of the play depict a total chaos of sound (files on microphones), images ('. . . horses and puss: hoarfrost and rats: eels and sicklebills'), and movements (flapping, wriggling), followed by absolute silence. Then, Kaspar pronounces Othello's despairing words, 'goats and monkeys', five times while the curtain, with progressively shriller sounds, jerks to a close toppling behind it the bodies of the five extra Kaspars.

The title *Kaspar* derives from the historical figure Kaspar Hauser, the 'wild boy phenomenon' who appeared on a public square in Nüremberg in 1828, able to utter only one sentence ('I want to become a horseman like my father was once'), and totally alienated from everything around him. Handke explained in an interview:

This Kaspar Hauser appeared to me to be a mythical figure, not just interesting as a simple case-history, but as a model of people who cannot reconcile themselves with themselves or with their environment, who feel themselves to be isolated.

Handke emphatically disclaimed any resemblance between the *real* Kaspar Hauser and his stage figure, and he warns the audience not to confuse the name Kaspar with any well-known 'tricksters', meaning Kasperl, German speaking countries' version of Punch. An 'over-life size Frankenstein' is Handke's preferred image of Kaspar.

Despite disclaimers, Handke does retain the title *Kaspar*, however, and uses quotations and paraphrases of material from the known accounts of the real Kaspar Hauser. In the play, the actual Hauser material relates to a 'private' world, which may predate the Prompters' text. This is significant as an alternate body of language relating to experience beyond the stage events. The evocative and emotive words relate to a private history (proscribed by the Prompters' text: 'You are normal once your story is no longer distinguishable from any other story'), and serve as a model for the uniqueness of any individual consciousness. Yet Kaspar, as anyone, has learned language, the Prompters being the chief teaching agents. Handke forces his critique to a logical, and mentally cramping, extreme, suggesting that structures embedded in language predate even the Prompters: to be conscious is to be stuck in grammatical tar. Handke's *Kaspar* poses problems in acute form of developing consciousness and socialization, the inseparable elements of human identity. The linguistic form he chose to deal with these problems coincided in the intellectual arena of Western Europe in the sixties with reawakened interest in structuralism and general sign systems. *Kaspar* is a semiotic treasure-trove.

Kaspar has an existence on stage before the Prompters

make themselves noticeable with *their* first sentence, 'Already you have a sentence with which you can make yourself noticeable.' He interacts with a strange environment and speaks his equally strange (to him) words: 'I want to be a person like somebody else once was.' The first movement of the play shows Kaspar, child-like, coming to grips with his world and attaining a state of self-awareness, marked in scene 14 by an abrupt silence which overcomes him.

Feeling alienated form his own limbs at first, Kaspar goes through the primary stage of learning by gradually gaining control of his physical being. While the Prompters cajole him with words about the practical uses and singular beauties of his sentence (chiefly to do with bringing 'order into every disorder'), Kaspar acquires confidence, and apparent mastery over the physical objects around him: he struggles free from a couch, throws a drawer to the ground, overcomes a chair (by removing its leg), nonchalantly trips a broom to the floor. At each turn he utters the sentence. At one point he is startled by the life in a freely moving object: a rocking chair. Handke was fascinated by the real Kaspar Hauser's inability to distinguish between things, animate/inanimate; two dimension/three dimension, etc. In Werner Herzog's 1974 film based on the Hauser legend, *The Enigma of Kaspar Hauser* (*Jeder für sich, oder Gott gegen alle: Each For Himself, or God Against All*), a light moment in the action occurs when Kaspar watches an apple skip over an outstretched foot. 'Clever little apple', he comments with a grin. Handke's Kaspar displays a similar primitive animism. The stage environment now in nearly complete disorder, Kaspar walks toward the remaining upright chair. Before reaching it something takes hold of him, and, now still, he can only say 'I want to be a person like'. The

accompanying words of the Prompters, and his own
growing self-awareness have seized him:

> You can hear yourself. You become aware.
> You become aware of yourself with the sentence.

The words continue in this vein, stressing 'learning and
order' and the stage darkens. Socialization and self
identity have begun.

In the next movement of the play, through to the
blackout at the end of scene 18, Kaspar has his sentence
'slowly but surely exorcised through the speaking of other
sentences'. Kaspar speaks parts of his sentence: phrases,
words, syllables, phonemes, then makes mere sounds while
the drone of the Prompters tortures him: 'Order. Put. Lie.
Sit.' Up to the point where Kaspar speaks his first new
'rational' sentence the Prompters jam his brain with words
directly and indirectly related to the physical environment
he has just mastered, and turned upside down. Kaspar's
words differ now, however, in that they begin to be
evocative. The German text is laid out in such a way as to
indicate that an actor might be 'trying to piece something
together', just as a person might try to piece together his
identity. The words conjure images of escape and terror:

> *He comes closer and closer to uttering a regular
> sentence*:
>> Into the hands.
>> Far and wide.
>> Or there.
>> Fell out.
>> Beat eyes.
>> No one is.
>> Goes neither home.
>> To the hole.

Goat eyes.
Reservoir.
How dark.
Pronounced dead.

If I myself already here at least tell.

By the end of this section, just before the blackout, Handke has Kaspar speak words which convey the sense of a personal history. They are a close paraphrase from Von Feuerbach's account of the actual Kaspar Hauser:

At that time, while I was still away,
my head never ached as much,
and I was not tortured the way I
am now that I am here.
(*It becomes dark.*)

Von Feuerbach: 'Kaspar said that at home (in his hole) he never felt so much pain in his head, and he was not tormented there as he is now in the world.' One doesn't need to know the Kaspar Hauser story to know that this language denotes a personal experience.

From this moment to scene 27 Handke demonstrates a learning and socialization process by having Kaspar put into words actions the audience has just seen him perform: 'After I came in, as I see only now, I put, as I see only now, the sofa into disorder . . .'. – a total of 13 'I see only now's', followed by 13 'Do remember that and don't forget it's'. Kaspar, with the guiding light of a spot, puts himself (ties, shoes, *etc.*) and his environment into order as the Prompters steadily indoctrinate him with 'self evident truths' derived from sources such as political platforms, books of household hints, handbooks of etiquette, 'folk wisdom'. The intended process of reification is apparent in this sentence of the prompters which reduces Kaspar to a grammatical unit; Kaspar is becoming, gradually, a mere sign in a larger system:

> The sentence about your shoelace and the sentence about you must be alike except for one word: in the end they must be alike to the word.

And the audience, now sharing Kaspar's verbalization of previous activities, is hypnotically drawn into the process of indoctrination by repetition. By the end of scene 27 the darkness which envelops Kaspar and his audience has a special significance: they join to contemplate the 'impossible image' freely created by Kaspar: 'black worms in the dark'.

Once taught 'the model sentences with which an orderly person struggles through life', Kaspar at the end of the scene speaks some thirteen lines simultaneously with the Prompters, for the only time in the play. For a moment, the 'speaking of someone else's text' is thus literally shown, as the Prompters induce Kaspar to internalize the text for which they in turn are only the agents of transmission. Aurally, this notion parallels the image of infinitely receding curtains on infinitely receding stages at the beginning of the play: the 'origin' of these systems, like language, is unknown. The scene builds with rapid alternation (26 of them) of 'you' (*du*) by the Prompters, and disconnected phrases by Kaspar, who continues to rock in his chair. The Prompters confuse Kaspar with contradictory sentences concerning the thought/speech continuum:

> When you begin to speak you
> will begin to think what you speak

even when you want to think something
different. Say what you think. Say
what you don't think.

Kaspar's chopped existential phrases in response ('When I
am, I was. When I was, I am. When I am I will.') lead up
to the desperate expression 'I am the one I am',
repeated three times. Kaspar stops rocking and, in a
paraphrase of a line from Ödön Von Horváth's *Glaube
Liebe Hoffnung* (*Faith Hope Love*) he creates an
'irrational' sentence, the question, 'Why are there so many
black worms flying about?' The image is one of despair, as
it is in Horváth's play, and might function here in a similar
fashion. But it has a further significance. First, as
mentioned above, the 'black worms' in the black space
shared by Kaspar and his audience are, in a sense,
impossible. Handke allows time to contemplate this by
calling for a pause in the dark. These words defy the
rational goal-oriented functioning of words. Words
demystify, fight back, as it were. There has been no
precedent in the teachings of the Prompters for such a
sentence as this. Precise lexical meaning is subordinate to
tone of response in later lines like the following:

PROMPTER: It goes without saying that despair is out of
place here;
KASPAR: It goes without saying that the flour sack strikes
the rat dead.

Kaspar may indeed be rebelliously 'talking back'.
Handke's open questions printed with the play in his
outline of Kaspar's thirteen phases of development allow
for such a reading: 'Can Kaspar defend himself at least
with an inverted world of sentences against inverted
sentences about the world?'

A real irony here, of course, is that Handke chooses for Kaspar's free 'creation', 'somebody else's' (Horváth's) text. The distinction between this and the Prompters' text, however, is that Horváth is classed as a poet, and Handke's Romantic system of values ranks artistic creation as constituting the genuine 'positive' history of mankind. A recent explicit statement of this idea appears in *Die Lehre der Sainte-Victoire*, (1980) (*The Teachings of the Sainte-Victoire*). Cézanne's painting a picture in 1904 constitutes an event of 'world import'. This idea of language and consciousness as double edged is basic to an understanding of *Kaspar*. The emptiness at the end of the play might betray a deep skepticism at the implicit thesis, but Handke, the enemy of all forms of control, resists with his play the normative dictates of all descriptions, from 'no elbows on the table' to 'kill every paradox'. As already mentioned, he tinkers with theatrical form and audience expectations too, possibly inducing the 'nausea at words' where new consciousness begins in those with the endurance to get through the play.

After Kaspar has been 'cracked open', as the Prompters put it, he remains mute for thirty short scenes. If the 'creation' of the sentence from Horváth registers a possible resistance through language, the immediate effects aren't particularly heartening. When Kaspar speaks again his words class him as an absolute model of conformity: 'I am healthy and strong. . . . I have already become used to everything. . . . I am prepared to be interrogated. . . . from now on I will be rational.'

Prior to Kaspar's pledge of rationality, while he is still mute, five 'look-alike' Kaspars appear. Their first function is to illustrate the laconic statements of the Prompters. Between blackouts, actions such as the following occur: 'Become aware that you are moving' (a Kaspar on crutches crosses the stage 'very very slowly', another one darts ahead of him, then back); '. . . everything falls back into order of its own accord' (a Kaspar pushes his fist into a cushion, it regains its original shape); 'Pains' (two matches are lit in the dark, then the lights come on, and the flames touch the Kaspars' fingers). Handke writes 'Neither Kaspar emits a sound'.

Alone on stage at the end of this section, Kaspar 1 performs a curious little mime. With exaggerated difficulty he forces one fist open with the other hand. Blackout. When the lights come up another Kaspar is sitting on the sofa. Kaspar 1, alone again after a blackout, 'spirals in on himself' and 'reaches for himself' before going to the closet and shutting it. Just before the intermission he leaves the stage, and 'the closet doors gradually open' of their own accord. These stage icons seem to relate to the same thing: opening, searching, shutting. They visually echo the distinctive line (it was marked as the *whole* of scene 31) 'You've been cracked open', which followed Kaspar's 'free' sentence and signalled his turning mute. The five extra Kaspars may well be extensions of Kaspar 1 (what comes out when he's cracked open), and at times as extensions of the world of the Prompters ('somebody elses', just like him, himself as socialized man). The image echoes others from the heyday of German Expressionist theatre. The actions of the five Kaspars, where they first appear, are to a large extent recapitulations of Kaspar's previous experiences on stage, as if Kaspar in his present mute state were visually re-thinking his own process of growing to consciousness and 'learning'. He seems to observe himself as an objective entity, rather the way he contemplated 'freely rocking' chairs at the start of the play.

After the interval, to the end of the play (scenes 60–65),

Kaspar 1 speaks through a microphone, signalling a capitulation to the Prompters. 'His voice begins to resemble the voices of the Prompters.' But the words he speaks, rendered less and less 'possible' by the mockery and interference of the extra Kaspars, return in the end to his personal history. First, song and rhyme are among the varieties of expression with which Kaspar colours his words, as he retells his stage history and repeats previous lessons: Kaspar, 'singing like a true believer', accompanied by the soft chant of his 'look-alikes':

No elbow on the table
no fish with the knife
no parasite
with the fingers
no spoon
with its side to the mouth
no solace for tired eyes
no truffles uncooked
every bum in jail:
kill every paradox.

To begin the penultimate scene all six Kaspars find relief in laughing at words. Kaspar repeats three times, 'Every sentence is for the birds' (in German, a rhyme is used: 'Jeder Satz ist für die Katz.') Then silence. What follows, for the rest of the play, is a mixture of Kaspar's retelling his stage history and his 'personal' history to the accompanying pandemonium created by the other Kaspars. They are physical outer embodiments of his inner skepticism at his own words, at the very fact that he uses language, and constitute a next stage of language awareness. The technique is expressionistic. One quiet passage begins: 'I can make myself understood,' and ends:

73

I have been made to speak. I have been converted to reality. – Do you hear it? (*Silence*) Can you hear? (*Silence*) Psst. (*Silence.*)

The last moments of the play, which have no correspondence to anything which actually happened on stage or which the Prompters said, bespeak a prior world or a world outside. The oblique references to 'snow', 'fear of the dark', 'sparkling objects' suggest experience which will not be blotted out, which Kaspar is condemned to utter in the language (form, not vocabulary) he has learned from his tormentors. That he becomes his own tormentor with this knowledge may constitute an ultimate despair in the play. 'If only, if only, if only' is softly repeated by the Prompters while the curtain shuts. The subjunctive mood, the form within a language that allows 'possibilities', may be the last subtle crushing touch in the 'speech torture' of Kaspar. And yet, for Handke, the act of creating the poetic myth *Kaspar* may be an act of muted hope.

George Steiner concludes his book on language and 'translation', *After Babel*, with a note on two versions of a Kabbalistic 'day of redemption' when the paradox of language will be resolved. According to one, 'All human tongues will have entered the translucent immediacy of that primal, lost speech shared by God and Adam.' According to the other, 'words will rebel against man. They will shake off the servitude of meaning. They will "become only themselves, and as dead stones in our mouths".' His summary lines apply to the dilemma of *Kaspar* and the art of Handke: 'In either case, men and women will have been freed forever from the burden and the splendour of the ruin at Babel. But which, one wonders, will be the greater silence?'[3]

5
Handke: 'The Ride Across Lake Constance' and 'They are Dying Out'

The premiere of *The Ride Across Lake Constance*, directed by Claus Peymann with the assistance of Wolfgang Wiens after an unsettled rehearsal period, took place in 1971 at the Schaubühne am Halleschen Ufer in Berlin. Among the production meeting remarks documented by Peter Iden are numerous references to a meta-theatrical approach to the play. Peymann called it 'the swansong of the bourgeois theatre', and the actor Bruno Ganz (who played Heinrich Georg) explained that the five central figures on stage, all named for stars from the classic German cinema, are essentially reflecting on their own activities as performers, 'objectively and not as signs' for something else. As in his other plays, Handke was directly engaged in an exploration of the form: but the audience could also witness in this 'laboratory piece', as its New York director Carl Weber called it, interpenetrating theatrical, social and personal realities.

Handke's prose text of the play, images flowing from one to the other by association of idea, is in a surrealist

75

dream mode. A later *The Weight of the World* entry states
the idea in personal terms:

> After last night's dreams: yet once more I believe in
> dreams – not in the sense that they express, mean or
> communicate something, but that they show a real and
> present other world which spans across the waking
> world and in which the people of the waking world
> reappear. . . .   (pp. 235–6)

In the nineteenth-century ballad which gives its title to
The Ride Across Lake Constance a Knight rides on
horseback across the frozen lake. Safely at the other side
he is told the ice is not more than an inch thick, whereupon
he drops dead. The thought of his recent danger, the very
words which inform him, are fatal. The 'mythic' aspect of
the ballad fascinated Handke, just as the Kaspar Hauser
'language myth' had done. The people in *The Ride Across
Lake Constance* find themselves caught in the interstices
between thought, speech and action, and are alternately
ecstatic at 'knowing where they are', and terrified by their
impotence. Occasionally there are also moments of respite
less ambiguous than Kaspar's brief 'free' creation of a
poetical phrase. A euphoria occasionally settles over the
figures in this play, a temporary acceptance of the fact of
things as they are, a momentary joy in a perceived
'harmony'. Obversely, they can also console one another
by enjoying the fact of their private petty confusions of
sense, or speech, or action. One wacky sequence ends in
song, sung in parts by the entire cast, to the melody of
'Whisky, Please Let Me Alone', in mock celebration of an
uncooperative chest of drawers. 'Let it be stuck', they sing,
implying that they also let jammed perception/cognition
channels be what they are, and absolute facts stand as they

stand, with no further pretension to significance than the elephant who passes water in the circus ring. They dance themselves silly, elegantly dodge one another (instead of clumsily crashing into one another) as they dart back and forth across the stage. When they settle, 'as in an after image', their release – 'We dreamed all that' – is the release from the need to be troubled by resistances: words, objects, unclear thought, faulty memory, the whole slop-bucket of consciousness. 'We forgot ourselves', they sigh, having achieved a momentary utopia. When Handke writes in his *Journal* that he has a need, at least once a day, to experience a sense of confusion – such as he felt the time he turned to see who was 'applauding' his window-washing efforts from the street below only to see a group of schoolchildren whose shuffling sandals on the sidewalk produced the 'applause' – he expresses the liberating side of a capricious sensory system. This is the opposite side of the coin to the shift in the radio play *Wind and Sea*, from perceiving neutral sounds (wind and sea) to threatening sounds (conflagration). Informing *Lake Constance* is another aspect of Wittgenstein's thought besides the purely linguistic, as expressed in his letter from the front in 1918: 'Our life is like a dream. But in our better hours we wake up just enough to realize that we are dreaming. Most of the time, though, we are fast asleep.'[1]

The style of *Lake Constance* alternates between lunatic farce and demonstrations of people in states of mental irritation and the numbness of fear. The individuals are subject to moments of panic, as when Emil Jannings evokes a 'bad moment' with words reminiscent of Kaspar's 'flying black worms': 'the maggot that crawls across the palm of the hand'. Handke expands the field earlier covered in *Kaspar* to include more people, more situations, more varieties of consciousness, once again foregoing the usual machinery of 'character' and plot. In his 1966 essay on circus Handke extols the virtues of that form for having no pretensions to being anything besides what it is; this 'absolute' performance quality is his elusive goal. Where illusion enters the play it is the sleight of hand of a good magician, a trick of perception. The first action of the play shows a maid in blackface, fresh from hoovering the room, 'lightly' and 'with a single movement', withdrawing a sheet from *under* the sitting Emil Jannings, after which a record player turns itself on signalling an awakening or a start for the play. And the figure Von Stroheim actually assumes the role of a stage *magician* at one point, mockingly and ironically demanding that his gestures be 'interpreted' by another character.

Certain basic premises of *Kaspar* are also evident in *Lake Constance*: a universal grammar threatens to govern the actions of his ordinary extraordinary five main characters. A 'dreamer' in the play, Elizabeth Bergner – 'I only walked into the parlor to turn off the light and have been lost without a trace ever since' – together with Henny Porten and Eric Von Stroheim enact a bizarre protracted social tango at one point, a parody of a love triangle, and an emotional equivalent of the theme of ownership and entrapment which runs through the play.

The effect is difficult to describe: rather like a grotesque set of Edvard Munch lovers come to life, or Strindberg in slow motion. One woman (Portner) guides the *other* woman's (Bergner's) hand under the man's (Von Stroheim's) vest. The *other* woman withdraws her hand quickly, as if shocked. But it is the first woman who shouts. The image of entanglement and displacement is literal. Handke apparently means all the parts of these gestures to be shown, hence the lengthy descriptions. The idea of incongruence between articulation and thought has shifted from the verbal to the visual. The image eventually extends to the whole set of five characters, who become the object of the very ritualized actions they are performing. The people themselves are like animated parts of some strange social grammar: an ultimate semiotic 'moment'. When Jannings kicks George he hardly moves, but at that very instant, Porten tumbles across the stage as if *she* had been kicked. Von Stroheim, dazed, sits with his one leg poised in the air ready to administer a kick. The stage direction reads: 'Startled, they all look at each other', and Bergner, as if she were not even in the play, makes the comment:

> It's nice to watch when something is beginning to function smoothly. It's like watching a sale: move after move. Here the goods, there the money! Here the money, there the goods!

The action proceeds by association of idea, with the motif of emotional/sexual possession weaving itself into that of the smoothly functioning sale. The automatic social response is equated to the automatic sexual response is equated to the automatic cash response, as it were. Spontaneity is dead. A typical Handke notebook entry reads: 'Somebody drops something and my hand leaps from its pocket, without me doing anything else'.

The last scene of the play gives an idea of the overall flow of action in *The Ride Across Lake Constance*. Handke quotes Shakespeare, rearranging the last line to suit his dramatic purpose:

> Am I in earth, in heaven, or in hell?
> Sleeping or waking, mad or well-advised?
> Known unto these, and to myself disguised:

Am I transformed, master, am not I?

(Comedy of Errors)

The lines could serve as an alternative motto to the play. *Both* the madcap humour *and* the terror (Shakespeare does not invoke witchcraft lightly) arising from total misunderstanding and disorientation which are at the core of Shakespeare's play characterize the final scenes of *The Ride Across Lake Constance.* Nature's very own surrealist joke, based on the laws of pure chance – identical twins – serves as the central living metaphor for Handke, as for Shakespeare before him. In *Kaspar*, Handke trotted out *five* replicas for the main figure. In the novel *A Moment of True Feeling* Keuschnig agonizes over the feeling that he may just be a double of himself. ('Do you ever wake up and find you've lost the connection?') It is no surprise that Peter Handke won the Kafka prize for fiction.

With the arrival at the end of the play of the Kessler twins, named for a popular song and dance team of the fifties, Handke signals a change in mood and perception: the characters seem to be 'waking up' as the stage light 'gradually turns to early morning light again'. They are returning to the 'waking' part of their dream.

The Kesslers drill the other characters into a euphoric acceptance of everyday formulas: 'Thanks,' 'Don't mention it,' 'But I insist.' They act out former images of displacement: using someone else's hand to fondle a third body. Von Stroheim finds himself with Ellen Kessler's leg thrust from behind between his legs. When Ellen speaks from behind, it is Alice in front who moves her lips. He can't move, he can't place the voices, in the end he can't speak, uttering only disjointed syllables. The spirit is pure Monty Python.

The last mime actions of Alice and Ellen Kessler

recapitulate the dichotomy which has established itself in the play: 'a bad day'/'things are going well'. First they work in parallel farcical harmony putting the room in order; then their movements 'begin to contradict each other', and everything the one does the other revokes: 'one dishevels the hair the other has brushed'. The Kessler interlude concludes with a final, stock slapstick joke: suitcases are thrown after them into the wings: no sound. Hats and gloves are thrown after them: sound of crashing suitcases.

Farce then gives way to terror. The source of the play's motto, Lessing's line 'Are you dreaming or are you crazy?' in *The Jews*, seems as appropriate here as Handke's version of it, 'Are you dreaming or are you speaking?' The two senses merge in such 'dialogue' as the following:

JANNINGS: Let us pray to God.
PORTEN: (*Insistently*): My candy.
BERGNER: (*In her sleep*): There's a rat in the kitchen.

In addition to these apparently private images of terror, their recent 'stage' history haunts the characters as well. The twins were exact biological duplications of each other. Now the characters are in danger of becoming exact 'performance' duplications of themselves. Jannings points for a match, tells George to get it, drops his hand, then suddenly screams 'NO!' when Von Stroheim reaches for the red cloth, as if preparing to give him another lesson as magician; Porten is questioned about motives, as she had been before. She screams, as if in mortal terror that the whole insane process were about to take grip of them again, whereupon the maid in blackface enters carrying a 'big doll that represents a CHILD'. The doll's 'mouth is enormous'.

One of the few American theatre groups Handke admired in the late sixties was German-born Peter Schumann's Bread and Puppet Theatre, whose (usually) over-life-size sculpted images came to transform notions of theatricality. Handke wrote in 1968 about the purity, simplicity and totally 'unreal' gestures of these puppet figures: 'lifting a hand is a story in itself'. They have a mythic aura about them, such figures, but need not signify anything specific. This is exactly the way Handke's doll functions: it howls, goes straight for the women's breasts and men's crotches, pauses momentarily when George shuts the drawer ('which was stuck', as they sang), tears the place apart, then withdraws. The doll, the maid, all of what has transpired cannot be rationally comprehended.

The dream world of the play unfolds itself into several present realities. Bergner has remained motionless through all the havoc of the doll scene. 'I only walked into the parlour to turn off the light and have been lost without a trace ever since' were her first words. To conclude the play, Von Stroheim leans towards her, her eyes open and she begins to smile. 'The stage becomes dark.' The rest of the characters have grown stiff and made themselves small 'as if freezing to death'.

Handke is working in an isolated area of Pirandello's charted country, at a more advanced juncture of the twentieth century when the speed-up effects of technology and communication have altered the mass consciousness and the intricacies of illusion. In his next play, *They Are Dying Out*, he was to explore similar areas of consciousness from the perspective of a single, articulate character – an urbane entrepreneur by the name of Hermann Quitt.

'They Are Dying Out'

Handke found Rainer Werner Fassbinder's 1974 Frankfurt production of *They Are Dying Out* (*Die Unvernünftigen sterben aus*: literally *The Irrational Ones Are Dying Out*) inadequate, 'distanced from my play'. Fassbinder had placed a set of elegantly attractive young actors on a stage covered with mounds of sand, through which they wandered uttering poetical melancholy statements of regret for a world of feeling which no longer exists. Handke explained that if he were to direct it himself he would stress that the characters are all quite different from one another, and not just aspects of the author's ego.[2] Peter Stein's Berlin production (1974) in which the fleeting connection between the main figure, Hermann Quitt, his wife, and a female business associate was underscored, Handke found closer to his own concept of the play. *They Are Dying Out* is a meditation on the possibility of experiencing genuine, spontaneous emotions (privately or with others) and of acting in unmediated accord with them. Motto to the play is Quitt's self doubting statement: 'It suddenly occurs to me that I am playing something that doesn't even exist, and that is the difference. That is the despair of it.'

They Are Dying Out ends in a scene of very stylized despair, extending the ideas of Handke's previous plays: a highly articulate and sensitive man destroying himself to the accompaniment of transcendent music, such as Beethoven's Freedom Chorus. In his final aria Quitt expresses the torment of his alienation, the fear that there is no unaffected self any longer, no 'free play' in his thought or life:

There is nothing unthought of any more. Even the Freudian slip from the unconscious has become a management method. Even dreams are dreamed from the beginning so as to be interpretable. . . . I wake up in the morning and am paralysed with all the speeches I've heard in the dream. There's no longer the 'and suddenly' of the old dreams.

In notes for producing the play, Handke asked for 'heavenly' music at the end. I asked Bruno Bayen about his 1980 Bremen production of the play and he explained that in conversation with Handke it had been decided to make certain changes. Bayen kept the idea of the suicide and the music, with changes in detail from the printed script, and added a slow dance by Quitt's wife and the servant Hans to accompany Quitt's demise. To end the play in Bremen, Bayen had Quitt murder the minority stockholder Kilb in the back seat of a Mercedes, then stuff his body in the trunk and direct the exhaust fumes into the car where he himself waited for the end, while Beethoven and carbon monoxide filled the stage. Hans and Frau Quitt danced on.

The 'plot' of *They Are Dying Out* concerns the powerful businessman, Hermann Quitt, who decides to transform himself, to break out of his role ('the old story with the masks', as someone in the play remarks) and give unhindered reign to the world of private feelings. Interestingly, Quitt's new subjectivity also entails adhering to old style, every man for himself, capitalist free enterprise. He betrays his business associates by refusing to enter a cartel with them, and by so doing threatens their financial empires. One by one the associates plead with him to reconsider, to no avail. The feelings of love, hate, loyalty, betrayal, once the staple of Shakespeare's royal

84

dramas, have been transposed to the world of technocratic cartel deliberations, according to Handke.

Hermann Quitt is in some ways an amalgam of both Kaspar and his tormentors, dressed in a business suit. He struggles out loud with the problem of his own conditioned responses, which of course he himself, directly and indirectly, has helped to create. He is at one time the perpetrator and the object of *Kaspar*'s 'speech torture', but in a very naturalized form. Ironically, it is his very penchant for the 'irrational' (poetry) that makes Quitt so successful in the field. He clearly holds his peers in awe. A mock line of imagery identifies him as a kind of Board Room Messiah: when they learn of his betrayal, one of the associates cries out 'Oh Quitt. Oh Quitt, why hast thou forsaken us?'

For all of the parody, however, there also seems to be genuine concern for the private agony of Hermann Quitt. Yet Quitt's talent for the poetic, admired even by his servant Hans, unsettles him. Handke directly involves the audience in Quitt's dilemma by evoking a response from a piece of literature from the previous century. Concluding the first act, just before Quitt makes his momentous decision to reject the cartel, Hans reads his master a lengthy passage from a story by the nineteenth-century Austrian writer Adalbert Stifter. In the story, *The Recluse*, the hero Victor grows to manhood, symbolically leaving his mother and his comfortable bucolic surroundings to visit his rich and eccentric uncle, the recluse of the title. Uncle and nephew concern themselves with matters of grave importance: ' . . . life is a limitless field if you look at it from the beginning, and is scarcely two paces long when you consider it from the end.' In the story, 'It seemed to Victor as if he had been dreaming for a long time and had only now returned to the world', when he finally leaves his uncle. The situation in Handke's play is comical: a fabulously wealthy businessman relaxes in an armchair while his servant reads him words from a time long past when genuine feeling, or at least the memory of it, was still possible. Yet the length of the quotation, and Handke's ambiguous attitude toward the world of Stifter's fiction, would indicate that he hopes to evoke some response from an audience – perhaps the 'memory of a feeling' – independent of the play. Stifter's prose is capable of inducing a tranquil emotional state despite, or maybe because of, its unaffected tendency towards sentimentality. The quotation is a rhetorical trick in *They Are Dying Out*, whose purpose is to edge the audience towards the state of feeling Quitt aspires to, and here, by this reading, artificially induces in himself: a sauna for the soul.

Directly after the 'reading', the tone shifts. Quitt, close to Handke's attitude, utters the line: 'anything that is meant to be serious immediately becomes a joke with me'. Soon after, thunder peals and Quitt 'emits Tarzan-like screams', announcing 'I want to get out of myself now. I am now myself and as such I am on speaking terms only with myself.' A quote from the past when feeling was possible has wrought a change in Hermann Quitt: his wife is reduced to inarticulate mutterings by the very presence of the new, one assumes 'private', man. Narcissism triumphant! The mockery and seriousness are inextricable. Handke once wrote that he envied Chekhov's talent for appealing simultaneously to the intellect and feelings. In *They Are Dying Out* he is trying to do so himself. Each of the other business associates in the play tries to persuade Quitt to change his ways – one through demonstrating a shared interest in 'poetical observations', one by trying to evoke sympathy, one, the 'businessman-priest' Koerber-

Kent, through fear. The latter predicts Quitt's death while dreaming will be 'gruesome beyond all imaginings'.

Most interesting of all Quitt's partners/competitors is Paula Tax, the 'Marxist businesswoman'. In the presence of the beautiful Paula Tax, emotion can jokingly mean simple motion for Hermann Quitt. While Koerber-Kent is still delivering his 'memento mori' pitch, Paula appears on stage and Quitt automatically unzips his fly. 'A garbage can cover bangs loudly on a hard floor backstage.' Paula describes the functioning of advertising, 'the only materialistic poetry', to Quitt who, she claims, wants to experience for all of us [like Jesus] what he experiences personally. Her dissertation is a parody of rational objections to Quitt's (Handke's?) defiantly 'private' stance. She defends advertising as concrete and rational, 'as distinct from bourgeois obscurantist poetry'. 'While the poets in their isolation conjure up something vague, the copywriters, working as an efficient team, describe the definite.' The results are also concrete: the phrase 'heaping teaspoon' instead of 'level teaspoon' increased sales by almost a hundred per cent.

While Paula Tax talks of awakening 'natural desires' she speaks as if she wants to 'avoid speaking of something else'. In his Bremen production, Bruno Bayen had Paula Tax subtly display herself as she stretched back in her chair while speaking of creamy substances. 'Do you like evaporated milk?' she asks, 'I suddenly feel like having evaporated milk.' The comical seduction ('My workers should never see me like this') operates on the very same principle of suggestion as the 'poetical' element in advertising. The scene is a good joke which dissolves into a typical Handke duet: 'She wraps her arms exaggeratedly around him . . . He throws himself on the floor and actually bangs his head a few times against it . . . their bodies touch. . . . [he] FLINGS her to the floor. She lies there, supports herself on one elbow.' Paula says: 'After your wife left I slowly exhaled . . . . (Loudly) As I exhaled, love set in.' In Act II, Quitt rejects Tax along with the rest:

PAULA: I'm going already. It's no use. I'll sell.

QUITT: (*Regards her*) And I'll determine the fine print. . . . Buying yourself a hat can be very comforting. . . .

PAULA: (*Suddenly embraces Quitt's wife, releases her, and tosses Quitt a friendly as well as a serious kiss as she walks out.*) 'No hard feelings . . .'

[English in the original]

Husband and wife stand opposite one another after Paula's exit, and the stage directions indicate a mélange of sound and light cues: sunshine, cloud, crickets, dogs barking, ocean sounds, child screaming in the wind, church bells, woolly tree blossoms blowing across the stage, the two figures thrown into silhouette while the noise of an aeroplane engine, first very close, recedes as the lights gradually return to normal – a reduction of a MOMENT OF TRUE FEELING to sheer parody. His wife softly says, 'You look so unapproachable.' The wife, of course, is a mere fixture in Quitt's world, something that shops.

Another type of relationship, between classes, exists between Quitt and his servant Hans. It is a conscious parallel to Puntilla and Matti in Brecht's *Puntilla and His Man Matti*. In the Brecht play, Puntilla the landowner only shows a human side when he is out of his senses, drunk. The servant is at the mercy of his master's whims, held responsible for Puntilla's lapses into humanity while under the influence. In the end, Matti leaves, self-assured, knowing that 'oil doesn't mix with water' and that each servant will be his own master. Nothing as straightforward as an awakening consciousness takes place in Handke's play. In the second act, Hans's words signal a change: 'I hereby announce that *my* world is changing'; and, 'I'm becoming human'. But the servant is wearing a chef's hat, sure that the filet will be left for him while he leaves his master to his fate ('he believes in things like that').

To open the second act, Handke has Quitt and Hans discussing the difference between the classes, as one experiences pity for them on stage. Quitt wonders why it is that he, who suffers by dint of his own articulacy, shouldn't be just as much an object of pity as the 'little people' whose inarticulacy drives them to violence in the plays one usually sees. The reference is a direct one to the characters in Kroetz's popular plays, and the servant's response could almost be Kroetz speaking: 'Even if you become speechless with suffering your money would speak for you, and the money is a fact and you – you're nothing but a consciousness.' In his 'derisive' rejoinder Quitt pleads for the right to see 'human beings on the stage, not monsters':

> Simple people, do you understand? Real people whom I can feel and taste, living people. Do you know what I mean? People! Simply . . . people! Do you know what I mean? Not fakes but . . . (*He thinks for quite a while.*) people. You understand: people. I hope you know what I mean.

When Quitt soon after says 'I meant that seriously', and laughs together with Hans while 'one of your real people' (the wife) enters, the ironical attitude parallels Handke's in the play as a whole. Handke's preposterous choice of an affected sensibility such as Quitt as a figure for anything like sympathy marks a daring choice of material. Whether the parody and irony can let up enough to allow sympathy to slip through is a delicate question answered only in performance.

At times, Quitt seems paradoxically to transcend himself even as he agonizes over his own lack of feeling. 'This aching lack of feeling, that was myself, and I was not only I, but also a quality of the world.' In the printed version of the play Quitt runs his head against a rock until he 'just lies there', and 'A fruit crate trundles down, as though down several steps, and comes to rest in front of the rock. A long gray carpet rolls out from behind the rock: snakes writhe on the rolled-out carpet and in the fruit crate.'

There is something comic-book grotesque about this ending. The theatrical receptacle overflows with images, sublime and vulgar, of states of consciousness: pre-verbal belches (when the minority stockholder enters), transcendent music, suicide as self-expression, arch quotations of SURREALIST images (Handke images) of the unconscious. The nausea at expressing, or trying to express oneself, even in art, is Handke's private dilemma.

6
Kroetz, Fassbinder and Drama for the Masses

Kroetz's success in relatively small theatres with plays like *Stallerhof* and *Ghost Train* proved not to be enough for a playwright interested in touching a mass audience. His first plays were grouped with those by Fassbinder, Martin Sperr and Wolfgang Bauer because of common features such as attention to specific milieus, stress on local dialect and slang, and concentration on small excerpts from reality. Kroetz has more than once expressed the opinion that his early recognition owed something to the wave of 'neo realist' plays at the end of the sixties. While Peter Handke had become an outspoken literary phenomenon, Kroetz on several occasions provoked public outcry with his work, and achieved a notoriety which went beyond the plays themselves. (In July of 1973 an Austrian high school teacher was fired without notice for arranging to read *Stallerhof* with her class.) In the course of the seventies Kroetz also frequently made open critical statements on the state of the nation and partook in party politics. His attitudes toward his work as a playwright changed significantly, though his approach to structure (short simple scenes) and realistic dialogue remained largely unchanged.

Following his commitment to Marxism Kroetz reassessed his early work, extensively revising some of it. Looking back on *Men's Business*, a battle in the 'war between the sexes' (his words) involving a female offal merchant in her mid-thirties, her pet dog, and a forty-year-old construction worker, Kroetz decided it presented 'cheap people cheaply'. In successive revisions (*A Man A Dictionary*, 1973; *He Who Through The Foliage Wanders*, 1976) he shifted emphasis from the surface rawness of the action (implied bestiality, coerced fellatio) to the private psychology of the woman, Martha, whose diary became a technical device on stage for her to articulate private fears and longings. The final version is the richest of the three, because of this emphasis on the individual.

With the new plays in this second phase of Kroetz's career, dating roughly from 1972, he tried consciously to break from a fixed writing scheme, concentrating on the problems of 'average' people, while also trying to present 'models' which showed 'paths to follow' or to suggest the 'vision of a better society' within the context of his social critiques. None of the pieces really descends to the woodenness of formula socialist realism, however. The later plays deal more explicitly with connections between personal and family crises and the larger pressures of society. Kroetz described as his 'special literary problem' trying to create plausible working and lower middle class characters who have a future. The West German families in his plays, rather like their American counterparts in early Arthur Miller (whose work Kroetz admires), struggle to retain an emotional equilibrium and a dignified sense of themselves under unrelenting social and economic pressures which they are hard-put to understand.

Kroetz was not alone in turning to this set of characters in the seventies, nor was he alone in trying to reach a mass audience through the media. 'The more viewers I have the happier it makes me,' he said in a 1973 interview, 'It's not a question of the medium, but the masses. Television offers the greatest number of viewers. . .'. Kroetz's *Upper Austria* (1972) and *The Nest* (1975) were successfully broadcast on television, and his adaptation of Josef Martin Bauer's *Mr. Adam Deigl and The Authorities* (*Der Mensch Adam Deigl und die Obrigkeit*), conceived as a film, also deals with the same general topic as his plays. In 1974 fellow Bavarian Rainer Werner Fassbinder produced a television series entitled *Eight Hours Do Not Make a Day* (Westdeutsches Rundfunk), only five of the eight parts of which were ultimately broadcast. Fassbinder's soap opera co-opts the television family series form, injecting unusual content into the story of a tool maker named Jochen. The intellectual perspective of Kroetz's plays from this period overlaps with that of Fassbinder, although the two authors had earlier had an altercation over Fassbinder's film version (1972) of Kroetz's play *Game Crossing*. Kroetz had taken Fassbinder to court accusing him of belittling the characters by inventing new prurient scenes and by sensationalizing the story of teenage sex and patricide with such images as the close-up of a penis. Kroetz's attempt to distance sensational material and to remove any 'cheapness' from his work in this case conflicted with Fassbinder's penchant for graphic melodrama and exotic imagery.

Fassbinder and Kroetz do bear comparison, though, especially for non-German readers. Fassbinder's play *Katzelmacher* (1969), adapted to film, depicts oppressive small town attitudes which form the same background as

Pig Headed and *Dear Fritz*, two early Kroetz plays. It depicts a fringe figure, a foreign worker, (*Gastarbeiter*) alienated from his antagonistic and resentful native hosts. In Fassbinder's film *Ali, Fear Eats The Soul*, (1973) a foreign labourer nearly establishes a mutually satisfactory relationship with an older washerwoman, but external pressures prove to be too great, and by the last scene he is in the hospital, suffering from acute stomach ulcers. The subtitle of the film indicates its characteristic irony: 'Happiness is not always fun'. Fassbinder avoids sentimentality in his melodrama by film techniques and often by a staginess in the acting and direction. His emphasis on short scenes, few words, hopeless fringe figures, makes his early work analogous to Kroetz's. He creates stylized tableaux from the real world, parallel to Kroetz's stage pieces.

Fassbinder's notes on *Eight Hours Do Not Make A Day* echo Kroetz's tone of voice on the subject:

> Nobody knows whether a family series is so called because it is about families, cherished by families, cherishes the notion of the family, or simply because it is watched by families. The reception of the family series is also controversial: the family loves it more than anything, the critic turns up his nose.

A typical episode depicts the problems faced by Jochen's group when their employer plans to change the plant's location. Though some welcome the idea (a shorter ride to work) the majority view it as a hardship. The group works towards how it might better organize its own labour and, in Fassbinder's words 'certainly a little is learnt about something'. Fassbinder's explanation for the type of series he conceived adequately describes aspects of Kroetz's work at the time:

1. *Rotter* by Thomas Brasch. The première in 1977 directed by Christof Nel with sets by Karl Ernst Hermann.

2. *Minetti* by Thomas Bernhard. Bernhard Minetti in the title role. Directed by Claus Peymann, Stuttgart, 1976.

3. *Minetti* by Thomas Bernhard. Bernhard Minetti in the title role. Directed by Claus Peymann, Stuttgart, 1976.

4. *Der Auftrag* (*The Mission*) by Heiner Müller with Jürgen Holz as Debuisson. Directed by Heiner Müller and Ginka Tscholakowa at the Theater im dritten Stock in East Berlin in 1981.

5. *Gross und Klein* (*Big and Little*) by Botho Strauss. Edith Clever as Lotte. Directed by Peter Stein in Berlin in 1979.

6. *Heimarbeit* (*Homework*) by Franz Xaver Kroetz from the premiére at the Werkraumtheater, Munich in 1971, directed by Horst Seide.

7. *Die Wahl fürs Leben* (*The Choice for Life*) by Franz Xaver Kroetz at the Munich Theater Rechts der Isar, in 1980.

8. *Die Wahl fürs Leben* (*The Choice for Life*) by Franz Xaver Kroetz at the Munich Theater Rechts der Isar, in 1980.

9. The set of *Nicht Fisch, Nicht Fleisch* (*Neither Fish nor Fowl*) directed by Peter Stein in Berlin in 1981.

10. *Kaspar* by Peter Handke. Directed by Peter Brook with the Centre International de Recherche Théâtrale, 1972. Presented in penal institutions on the outskirts of Paris.

11. *Ritt über den Bodensee* (*The Ride across Lake Constance*). Directed by Claus Peymann and Wolfgang Wiens.

12. *Der anachronistıche Zug* (*Procession of Anachronisms*) by Bertolt Brecht. Hanne Hiob Brecht in the background.

When workers' problems are presented in television plays, it is often said that social criticism is taking place here. This wording reveals quite clearly enough that the films mostly appear to be sad, grey, acquiescent. As sincere as this sympathy with the workers as the betrayed members of this society may be, it is, at the same time, fraudulent, because following dramatic logic the miserable traits are permanently attached to the workers, traits which they seem to need in face of their wretched conditions.[1]

In *Eight Hours Do Not Make A Day*, as in Kroetz's plays, the author presents material 'not so much about the social conditions to which the workers are exposed, as about the possibility of living in these conditions – or changing them. These conditions are, however, from the point of view of those concerned, very concrete; it is about wages, the pressure of output, work conditions. . . . Certainly all these are part of "society" but not in the emphatic sense of a theoretical category, but in their special and realistic manifestation.' In Kroetz's *Adam Deigl* film the pressures referred to here are extended beyond the framework of the home environment to include scenes at the workplace, in court, and so on, while the 'realistic manifestations' in the stage plays are centred on the effects of the larger pressures on domestic situations. The best examples of this kind of play are the trilogy of 'folk plays', *Upper Austria*, *The Nest*, *Mensch Meier* and the related play *Big Max*. The first two of these plays were shown successfully on television.

In *Upper Austria*, Kroetz presents the dilemma which faces Anni, a saleslady, and her delivery-truck-driver husband, Heinz, when Anni becomes pregnant. Kroetz relates Heinz's specific worry, triggered by the idea of having a baby, to a general feeling of unease about himself: there is no freedom for him, 'too little time between working hours', and behind the wheel it is 'as if I weren't me at all, as if I were someone or other who had no meaning at all'. An unexpected pregnancy is familiar from Kroetz's earlier plays, but here the greatest emphasis resides in the financial strain which affects the stability of the couple's relationship, and inevitably opens areas of conflict not previously apparent. In the end the couple agree, tentatively, to have the child.

The Nest begins with a commentary from within the play itself on the purpose and desired effect of these folk plays about people whom Kroetz, in the tradition of Horváth and Fleisser, calls his 'little people'. The first scene opens with a TV announcer's statement that 'The play you have just seen was *Upper Austria*, by the Bavarian playwright Franz Xaver Kroetz in a production by the Heidelberg Theatre.' In view of the public controversy over the first broadcast of *Upper Austria*, which had been cancelled at the last minute because of Kroetz's intention to air a critique of the play directly following it, with the director Dieter Braun, a critic, and two 'audience representatives' whose political views were close to those of Kroetz, the reference to the first play is especially ironic. The broadcast of the Heidelberg premiere had been planned by ZDF (Zweites Deutsches Fernsehen: Second Programme) for 25 April 1973, with the previously taped discussion to follow. The censors argued that the discussion strayed too far from the play itself – implicitly that it was too political. In August 1973 the play was broadcast, without the discussion.

The couple in *The Nest* are happily preparing for the birth of their child, mother-to-be Martha doing sewing for extra money while she watches *Upper Austria* on TV. Kurt and Martha talk about the TV play, remarking that their situation is quite different. After all, the husband there was only a delivery man, not a proper truck driver; 'and anyway it's not normal for a man to be afraid of his child'. Though Martha dismisses the piece as unrealistic, she responds directly to it, as Kroetz would hope other viewers might do: 'I'd have fought for my child too.'

The crisis in *The Nest* occurs after Kurt performs a special assignment for his boss, emptying eight barrels of 'brownish red fluid', purported to be sour wine, actually a dangerous chemical, into a lake. Just after Kurt dumps it at the clandestine family swimming area, his wife unknowingly takes their child into the water. The boy eventually recovers from his burns, and the melodrama ends on a note of hope as Kurt (accused by his wife of being no better than a 'trained monkey') recognizes the need to resist his masters: 'The Union, that's something big.' His personal authority over the wife and child correspondingly relaxes too. Kroetz's message is simple, and clear.

In the best of the trilogy plays, *Mensch Meier*, all three characters are more complex, and involved in ambiguously developing relationships. The mother and father, Martha, a housewife, and Otto, an auto-assembly-line worker, both 'around forty years old', face personal crises at the same time as their fifteen-year-old son, Ludwig. As in Kroetz's other plays, 'normal' family structures as they exist in and reflect social and economic structures are called into question.

The frustration and alienation experienced by the breadwinners in *Upper Austria* and *The Nest* is apparent in all three figures in *Mensch Meier*. The title itself is a pun, one meaning of which is the reference to the everyday expression of exasperation which one can overhear on any street in Bavaria: 'Ach, Mensch Meier, ich habe schon wieder den Schlüssel vergessen!' ('Oh, for crying out loud, I forgot my key again!'). The 'Meier' part of *Mensch Meier* refers to the genus Meier: the 'Jones' or 'Smith' of Bavaria, a kind of 'Loman'. And 'Mensch', among its other connotations, literally means 'human being', something all of Kroetz's 'little people' would prefer to be than 'trained monkeys'. Other Kroetz titles have a similar function: aside from obvious puns, like *The Nest*, and references to proverbs as in the titles for the rewrites of *Men's Business*, Kroetz anchors his titles to the everyday by choosing common phrases from a variety of sources: *Weitere Aussichten* (*Future Prospects*: about the plight of a woman at the threshold of entering a retirement home) appears in all weather report sections of the newspapers; *Der Stramme Max* (*Big Max*) refers to heartiness and bravado strength in general, but is also a favourite working man's lunch of ham and cheese on black bread which appears on most Bavarian menus. This local reinforcement of image and idea is one of Kroetz's strategies as a writer.

The three Meiers share a feeling of being trapped, by family and social circumstances. Ludwig is naturally at the bottom of the family pecking order, accused by his father of being out of work because he is lazy, and at the same time forbidden to entertain thoughts of becoming a manual labourer: along with Heinz in *Upper Austria* and Kurt in *The Nest*, the *pater familias* in *Mensch Meier* is determined to have his son improve the stock, maybe by becoming a dental technician. At one point, Ludwig sarcastically follows this logic and remarks that *his* son will have to be Bundeskanzler at least.

Scenes depicting Ludwig's pointless daily life, begging for small change from his father and proving his worth by shining shoes (Otto teaches him how to do it 'right'), eventually give way to others in which he confronts his parents and leaves home to become an apprentice mason on a job site. Martha's independence is also restricted in a familiar way, until she recognizes the humiliation of having been nothing much more than shopper, household servant, and oddly, a substitute sex object in Otto's fantasies. He says he sometimes prefers just to buy pornography and masturbate. She leaves, takes a menial job selling slippers, and lives in a rented room. She knows Otto will always remain what he is, so despite occasional meetings, she can see no point in a reconciliation. Ironically, considering the theme of 'speechlessness' in Kroetz's first plays, Martha's reason for secretly moving to a second rented room at the end of the play is so she can avoid being pestered by her husband who insists on visiting her uninvited, and discussing things 'for hours on end'. Martha's 'liberation' is hardly unambiguous, since she has really exchanged one form of economic dependency for another.

Otto's case is similar to the other males in the trilogy in that his conventional position of power in the family is predicated on secure financial control. Lay-offs and increased work load, felt acutely by Otto because a close friend (the 'only' one, Martha says) is fired, eat their way into his imagination causing the same nervous symptoms experienced by Heinz and Kurt. One phenomenon which distinguishes Otto from the other two workers, however, is the extent to which Kroetz has developed his fantasy life. Otto makes and flies model aeroplanes as as hobby, and Kroetz shows him in several scenes, alone, genuinely enjoying himself. In the first act he fantasizes both parts of an imagined TV interview: as a great model plane expert who has gone from a 'mere worker' to the point of mastering the 'long distance flight' and eventually owning 'a sort of little factory, turning the hobby, so to speak, into a profitable occupation'. The scene shows an important side of Otto which has been repressed, and his childish apprehension that he may be discovered while fantasizing in this way stresses the point. For Kroetz the final absurdity is that Otto aspires to be a small time factory owner. He underscores the idea that Otto's actual work, inserting fourteen screws in the windshield of a BMW (plus two in the door, after the lay-off of other workers), does not allow for creativity, by showing him in his private life enjoying a technological hobby.

The play is constructed in scenes of varying length, but none lasting more than about ten minutes; Kroetz can thus contrast aspects of Otto's life relatively simply, without need for lengthy comment. For example, he follows one very funny scene (titled 'memories') in which Otto and Martha nervously worry over having been short-changed in a restaurant, by another ('mountain climber') in which Otto flies his plane out in the open. He looks up and says: 'Up there you're free.' In his 'reportage', *Chiemgauer Gschichten* (1977), Kroetz asked an East German worker if he had the choice between quitting the Communist Party or giving up model plane flying which he would do. The answer was quit the party. Many of the details in these closely observed plays probably have their origin in such anecdotes.

When Otto's world begins to fall apart, after he is separated from his wife and son, the fantasy Kroetz has established for the character allows him to express his mood of alienation in richer language. In Act III, scene 3 ('mirror mirror') Otto is again alone, watching a 'What's My Line' TV show, speaking to himself while the moderator talks:

What am I? . . . I'm an asshole. How's that? What are
you? I'm an asshole. Skilled or unskilled? . . . [I] screw
sixteen screws into a BMW 525. Car manufacturer? Yes.
Carscrewscrewer, screwscrewer, screwschoolboy,
screwologist. Are you perhaps a screwdriver? How's
that? Mr. Lambke, is the candidate a screwdriver? Yes
indeed, the candidate is a screwdriver. If you would be
so kind, Mr. Meier, to show us your hands. Only too
gladly. You see before you, dear audience members, the
distinguished [*ausgeprägte*] screwing hand with three
fingers and the other with two fingers. This reduction is
the result of breeding. The remaining fingers are double
the size of normal fingers and are optimally suited to the
work operation.

Each character's need for independence and freedom
ironically forces him into isolation. At the very end of the
play mother and son meet briefly and talk, deciding that
they have made certain choices for themselves and now it is
the father's turn to 'learn' something.

LUDWIG: And Papa?
MARTHA: (*shrugs her shoulders, quietly*) Has to do it
    too.
LUDWIG: What?
MARTHA: What we're doing. Learn.
    END

An important feature of *Mensch Meier* which makes lines
like the ones just quoted quite plausible is the actual
texture of a family life which Kroetz creates.

The Modernes Theater in Munich has staged numerous
Kroetz plays in close association with the author. Their
production of *Mensch Meier* (1980) will give a sense of his

play on stage in his native Bavaria. Ludwig wants to borrow fifty marks to go to a rock concert, and when he can't cajole his father into giving it to him he steals it. Otto and Martha then face the embarrassment of coming to the grocery store check-out counter short of money. Otto blusters and abandons his wife in the store. The following scene shows Otto callously humiliating his son, forcing him to strip naked in the search for the missing fifty mark note. In the Modernes Theater production the mother and son displayed a mute strength through this scene, auguring their future determination to change things, while Otto grew more terrifying and pathetic as he ranted like a sergeant major. Martha's line, deliberate and cold, 'I'll never forgive you', and Otto's answer, 'Why?', spoke volumes about their 'model' relationship and set the tone for her 'rebellion', as a later scene title describes it. When Georg Tressler, director of the Modernes Theater production, wrote about the strength of Kroetz's play he called it a 'folk play in the truest and most modern sense – filled with humour, bitter, sometimes quite hard and always evocative'.

As directed by Tressler, the second scene in the play ('with guests') gave a concrete sense of lived experience on a Saturday afternoon watching television. In the short humorous scene Kroetz unobtrusively prepares for all of the tensions and confrontations to come. The program they watch is a 'live' account of the wedding of the ordinary German girl, Silvia Renate, to the King of Sweden. Predictably, the son, Ludwig, named for Bavarian royalty himself, is cynical and bored: he chants at intervals the words 'hunger' and 'boring', and resents having his lunch delayed while mother watches the wedding festivities. The display of wealth impresses Otto, who makes jokes about the bride's prior state of virginity and her ability to 'trap' a man, and expresses some discontent when demonstrators apparently interfere with the celebration. Martha shares her husband's upset at the disruption, for she sees the royal wedding as a 'fairly tale' event, like her own wedding. Otto's awed remark on how much the 'whole circus' must cost is natural enough, and in the Meier family situation leads to inevitable carping about his son's inability to earn money. Kroetz's critique of conditions in the world where those who do absolutely nothing live off the labour of others is quite plausibly wound up in the domestic squabbling of the Meier family. Otto comments on the demonstrators at the wedding:

OTTO: They don't like red flags. (*Nods.*)
MARTHA: That's not right at a wedding, regardless of the politics behind it.
OTTO: Sweden.
MARTHA: Exactly.
LUDWIG: Hunger.
MARTHA: Listen to that one, just like he brought in the money we live off! I'd like to see that!
OTTO: Earn something, then you'll get something. Precisely!
LUDWIG: Right.

In Tressler's production the very basic comment about 'hunger' and 'earning' in the larger context, was physicalized locally and with great humour by punctuating the dialogue through these scenes with minor skirmishes over the pretzel bowl. By the end of the play, Ludwig leaves home to do just what his father and mother insist: earn a living, though not as a 'professional' as they would have it. (In *Chiemgauer Gschichten*, Kroetz says he was thinking of having the son in *Mensch Meier* be in a

Socialist Youth organization, but decided not to. 'I can see now how the bourgeois press will react: agitation, improbable . . .'.) And Martha, here enchanted by the romance of fairy tale weddings, will eventually be forced to see the reality of her own domestic and personal servitude. While mother and son take a tentative step forward, Otto by the end of the play still can't distinguish between 'Sweden', as it were, and his own present reality. What makes *Mensch Meier* the best of Kroetz's trilogy plays is that he doesn't allow theme or idea to dominate as such.

Kroetz's next two efforts in the 'folk play' mode, *Big Max* (1978) and *Neither Fish Nor Fowl* (1980), continue in the vein of *Mensch Meier*. Both are more explicitly critical of actual working conditions which affect his blue collar characters. The title character Big Max suffers ill health caused by the polluted environment of his workplace, a chemical factory, and Kroetz contrasts this unacknowledged peril to national attitudes toward 'war sacrifice'. Max's naiveté early in the play is shown as he sits on the company toilet and reads a leaflet describing unhealthy factory conditions: 'Communists behind this,' he mutters to himself, using the leaflet as toilet paper.

Neither Fish Nor Fowl, which had simultaneous 1981 premieres in Düsseldorf and at the Schaubühne am Halleschen Ufer in Berlin, directed by Peter Stein and designed by Karl-Ernst Hermann, indicated the road Kroetz has travelled since his humble beginnings on studio stages a decade earlier. I asked Kroetz just after he had written the play whether he had ever hoped to have his 'folk' plays performed by local Bauerntheater (rustic folk theatre) groups where the audiences might be of the same class as the characters in the plays. He said one problem would be that his plays are too difficult for the local groups to produce adequately. If he had full control of a theatre for a five-year period some time, as Intendant, he could work to change the social makeup of theatre audiences, but since that is not likely he is content to find the best directors and actors possible for his premieres, and then to hope for mass exposure in radio, television and film. Kroetz has in the past few years been regularly directing and acting in the media as a way of extending his experience and knowledge of those forms.

The Berlin production of *Neither Fish Nor Fowl*, according to critic Henning Rischbeiter (*Theater heute*), showed that the efforts by Kroetz in this play to expand his vision beyond the customary realism were not fully successful, at least as interpreted by director and designer.

There are two couples in the play, friends whose personal and professional dilemmas parallel and contrast with one another. Couple number one, Edgar and Emmi, are, respectively, a typesetter and a saleslady. In the course of the play he becomes the victim of advanced technology, when computerized photographic type setting is introduced, and will have to 'retrain'; while she is promoted to branch manager by her employers. The wife wants a career, her husband a family. Just the opposite orientation exists for Hermann and Helga, as she resents the attention he gives to labour issues and union work: his outspokenness has cost him several jobs already, and gradually alienated him from herself and the children. Consecutive scenes which open the play, each couple in bed, present in the simplest terms the interrelationship of work and personal life: neither Emmi nor Hermann are inclined to respond sexually to their partners, preoccupied as they are with their jobs. 'Shit on emancipation', says Edgar, only half jokingly; and Helga wishes her husband would learn to keep his mouth shut and hold a job so they can live in peace.

Fantasy and freedom of imagination share a considerable role in Kroetz's most recent plays. One can almost hear an ironic echo of Handke's businessman soul-searcher Hermann Quitt in Edgar's desire to find 'a new me, whom no one knows'. Edgar's hobby, an aquarium of tropical fish where 'nature reigns' and 'big fish eat little fish', serves as a means of escape for him, and Kroetz weaves the hobby as a metaphor into the thematic material of the play. In Act II Edgar and Hermann obliquely share their frustration:

> EDGAR: Take away my profession and you take my life and chuck me in the water. I'm not a very good swimmer and when I dive I don't get any air. (*smiles*) Even though I'm a Pisces.
> HERMANN: Me neither.

Towards the end both men pack to leave, Edgar first performing a grotesque mime in the kitchen which he has just cleaned, 'almost pedantically'. He takes a teddy bear into the kitchen, and with an electric drill bores a hole between its legs, inserts a carrot, whittles the carrot to a stump, fetches a handkerchief, puts it on the table, splotches it with red wine, takes a piece of string and ties the handkerchief around the piece of carrot, makes a knot, takes out the scissors to cut off the end of the string, sets the bear erect, cleans up, takes his hat, goes, and throws the key back in. The penultimate scene shows Edgar undressing slowly, water somewhere near, while Hermann crawls onto the stage, complaining that his colleagues have inflated him with air – literally, with a car pump up the rectum. Edgar invites his friend to go with him, presumably into the water, but Hermann refuses:

HERMANN: Mankind. (*yells, farts*) Man! (*turns around and crawls at a snail's pace away from the bank to land.*) Mankind, it takes a while, something has to come of it, something stinks.

EDGAR: I'm in already.

HERMANN: Can't swim.

EDGAR: (*further away*) Lies!

Karl-Ernst Hermann's setting for this scene came to life apparently, in the form of metre long fish which were inflated on sections of the stage. Critic Henning Rischbeiter wondered whether it was just unintentional comedy or an adequate extension of the neo-expressionist aspects of the scene, concluding that what is good in *Neither Fish Nor Fowl*, in the 'new' Kroetz, is not the expressionism but rather the familiar 'old' Kroetz, who as an 'ultra-realist' shows the pressures on average people, their attempts to overcome and break out of their situations, and the relapse into normality. The concluding scene of *Neither Fish Nor Fowl* shows the two women at a table, Hermann suffering from stomach cramps, as Edgar enters, half naked. He says 'I'm cold', and Helga offers him soup.

7
Kroetz: The Search for New Forms

During the period when the trilogy of folk plays appeared Kroetz was also trying to expand the formal range and subject matter of his work by adapting classics from the German theatre and by studying the techniques of Brecht.

Of his two Friedrich Hebbel adaptations, *Maria Magdalena* (1972) and *Agnes Bernauer* (1976), the latter, which strays further from its original, is the more successful. Kroetz converted the fatalistic *Maria Magdalena* (1844) about the conflict between conventional morality and a struggle for sexual freedom of its middle class heroine, into a grotesque comedy, which unfortunately relies too much on knowledge of the original for full effect. Maria's suicide in Hebbel's play, a demonstration that the tragic emotion is not reserved for the aristocracy, becomes an off-hand joke in Kroetz, who in part intends to debunk the middle class itself. Maria announces 'I took poison', and her father, engaged in cards, dismisses her with the words, 'Don't play games'. In

Agnes Bernauer satire gave way to a psychological approach to character.

In Hebbel's *Agnes Bernauer* (1852) Albrecht, heir-apparent to a Bavarian dukedom, is in conflict with his father Ernst, over the younger man's love for an eminently worthy girl from the wrong social class. When Agnes is drowned as a witch, Albrecht begins to see the rightness of his father's decision. The individual matters little to tradition and to the state machinery, and her death is a tragic by-product of historical necessity. In his play Kroetz disregards most of the details of the original in order to focus on the psychology of the main character caught up innocently in historical circumstances.

Ernst Werdenfells in Kroetz's play owns a very successful rosary bead assembly firm in a small Bavarian town, which he controls by employing local villagers at low wages. In Zola-esque contrasts, Kroetz describes the cleft between the castle life of Werdenfells and his family, and the drudgery in the cottages. Agnes Bernauer, daughter of a bankrupt barber, is determined she will not have to stoop to piece-work slavery, so she sets out to ensnare the young Albrecht Werdenfells, and succeeds. In the course of the play she and the weak-minded Albrecht undergo a transformation of thinking and feeling. By the end Agnes gives up her security to throw her lot in with the poor. The play, which began with one funeral (Agnes's mother), followed by another (Albrecht's dog), ends in muted hope with the birth of Agnes's child. In the birth scene, at the workers' lodgings, the terrified Albrecht unintentionally tears open a bundle of rosary beads, creating a great stir, then the play closes on this sentimental note:

GIRL: What is it?
GRANDFATHER: One grubber more. [the baby]

109

AGNES: (*softly*) Albrecht?
ALBRECHT: (*smiles*) I'm here.

The melodrama of this closing moment is typical of *Agnes Bernauer*, and oddly, represents one of its strengths. Kroetz succeeds in presenting raw emotional conflict of a personal sort which, presumably, is meant to speak for larger, class conflicts. The individual scenes are convincing, and quite different from Kroetz's low-key style in his other works. Agnes must wrestle with the Werdenfells family for possession of Albrecht, who well knows 'Your thinking is going to kill us'. She forces the entrepreneur to recognize himself as an exploiter, and induces him to give an apologia – and a fairly convincing one at that – for his behaviour. Werdenfells's arguments are those of the 'economic miracle' generation – we suffered hard times, we earned it on our own. With Werdenfells, Kroetz partially succeeds in creating a character from the 'other' (non-Marxist) side, something he felt had been lacking in earlier plays. But Agnes's sarcastic response to Werdenfells's denial of responsibility could be a direct comment by Kroetz on social inequity: 'and the hard times, now force them onto others, right?'.

The change in Kroetz's writing technique can be seen in the second act where Bernauer, Agnes's father, stinking drunk, gives himself a haircut and emerges dripping with blood, 'like Jesus Christ'. A financial and spiritual bankruptcy tells in bizarre imagery here, as Werdenfells, with lines like 'money heals all', settles a four-hundred mark per month pension on the unfortunate failure. Bernauer is not so wounded, however, he cannot haggle for more, adding a comic touch to the scene.

Later in the play Agnes, referred to as an 'angel', goes to the fair and distributes free tickets for the rides to all

present. The young people think she has gone mad, but
accept her offer. The collection of working class youths
steadily grows wild, however, tearing her clothes off and
leaving her prostrate. Kroetz succeeds thereby in subduing
any facile attitude about the masses or about Agnes's
'charity' at that point. In the parable style of the play – she
does resemble Grusha of *Caucasian Chalk Circle* or Shen
Te of *Good Woman of Setzuan* – the scene functions well.
A fairground ride operator who also exploits Agnes
comments: 'Goodness doesn't pay. I could have told you
that before'. Kroetz does deliver judicious little sermons
on the workings of (as it appears in this play) crude early
capitalist economy, perhaps with the hope of conveying
the information to a mass audience should the play reach
television. (It was premiered in 1977 in East Germany.)
Without the homilies, however, the acted images and
personal relationships themselves tell a simple and
effective tale.

After his first few years of success, Kroetz also studied
Brecht for the first time, having previously dismissed his
work, as was fashionable in the late sixties, in favour of
that of Horváth and Fleisser. Kroetz had then claimed that
Brecht's dialogue was not based on real speech. He
claimed to have started reading Brecht seriously in 1973,
but it wasn't until 1975 that he published anything
substantial on his work. Some techniques in plays written
in this period, chiefly the use of song, show similarity to
Brechtian ideas, but the dramaturgic centre of his plays
continued to be empathy. In *Agnes Bernauer* the tendency
toward parable associated with Brecht could be seen,
however, as could a new understanding of 'realism', which
went beyond description of situations and became more
'speculative'. He himself has said that direct comparisons
of his own work, or anyone else's, for that matter, to that

of Brecht, would be fruitless. As a result of Kroetz's explicit commitment, however, he was determined to experiment with several types of plays which break up the realistic flow of action and allow for direct political and social commentary.

In the two agit-prop plays, *Global Interest* (*Globales Interesse*, 1972), written on the occasion of the 1972 Olympics, and *Munich's Children* (*Münchner Kindl*, 1973), Kroetz has made his most direct political statements. The latter play, subtitled a 'Bavarian Ballad', presents the result of research on the subject of land speculation and rent profiteering, using a variety of documentary theatre techniques. The information is foremost in the play, though Kroetz provides a small family unit to respond, emotionally and rationally, to the information. What begins as idle curiosity on the part of the head of the household about the subject of profiteering, ends with him singing directly to the audience: 'How many will we be tomorrow? Defend yourselves.' Kroetz has stated that the writing of these agit-prop plays was important to him personally, presumably because they represented an active step in making his art useful in a direct way to his political cause.[1]

Both *Lienz: City of the Dolomites* (*Dolomitenstadt Lienz*) (1972), about prisoners in a provincial jail, and *Pennies From Heaven* (*Sterntaler*) (1976), which depicts the life of a father, mother and son after they have migrated from East to West Germany, are essentially realistic empathy-based plays, but through the use of song Kroetz allows his characters to present aspects of themselves directly to the audience, and he provides a gloss on the private aspects of their situations by giving information in the songs about the larger social context.

As the fairy tale title of the play suggests, Kroetz is

working in the mode of morality tale in *Pennies From Heaven*. Written at a time when his criticism of the West was at its sharpest, the play at first seems a naïve statement of faith that things were really better for this family in East Germany. In fact it is more complicated than that. Kroetz's scenes of melodrama and open sentiment have similarities to Fassbinder's films, and like them ask more questions than they choose to answer. What these average people are searching for is 'freedom', but the simple border-crossing, Kroetz suggests, will not provide that.

For the father, who most often repeats the notion 'we should have stayed', freedom translates to his abandoning the family and going to live in workers' quarters. The mother drudges on, fully confident that her efforts will pay off, only to be disappointed by the end of the play. Their son, Karli, infected with ideas of getting rich quick in the West, dies from a police bullet, in a sadly real 'gangster movie' scene (his favourite viewing) come to life. *Pennies From Heaven* is an uneven play, but does manage to raise important German (East/West) issues in domestic dramatic form.

Lienz: City of the Dolomites, subtitled 'Farce with Songs', in reference to Nestroy's favourite dramatic form, was the first published and produced Kroetz play to experiment with techniques to break up the realistic action, and can serve as an example of his use of 'Brechtian' techniques. The play deals with two hours in the lives of three prisoners, and from the layout of the script (some of the pages are actually blank) it is clear that Kroetz wants long silences and periods of inactivity to accentuate the boring reality of prison life. At the end of the play, the youngest of the three, Dengk, goes to the toilet while his cellmates Rasch and Schuster play chess.

HERIBERT DENGK: You playing chess. I'm going to take a shit.

HERMANN RASCH: Again?

OSKAR SCHUSTER: Cuz he's hungry.

HERIBERT DENGK: Cuz I don't feel so hot.

Dengk leaves, and the others play chess. He flushes the toilet several times, then it grows silent and remains that way for some time. They call him and when they get no answer, rush to find him on the floor of the screened-off toilet. Once they've panicked to his satisfaction, Dengk jumps up from the floor to say it was all a joke. Dengk's suicide prank is Kroetz's light handed way of stressing a serious theme, which has been present from early in the play. After Schuster and Rasch scold Dengk for risking getting all three of them in trouble, they return to play chess – the last full three pages of acting script have only the words 'chess-playing' printed on them.

Kroetz adds another dimension to the realistic depiction of alienation among his three prisoners by the use of songs which break the illusion of prison reality created by scenes like the one above. Heribert Dengk, in jail for car theft, has known the inside of institutions since his childhood in an orphanage. One of his songs, the 'Song About Home' tells the sad tale of Princess Caroline whose strict boarding school in England 'is not really a home' to her. The convicted cheque forger Hermann Rasch, whose childhood was marked by parental abuse, also sings about class divisions and injustice in his 'Song of the Average', about the 'engineering graduate with plans for the future'. The refrain informs us that those who make five thousand today will be making ten tomorrow, while those with five hundred will soon have nothing at all.

The eldest of the three, Oskar Schuster, expresses a pride

in himself when he tells the story of having repaired a coffee machine at the Radio Liberty studio where he once delivered bread. 'It'll still be working', he says, and 'Maybe they all watched me fixing it. A small sensation.' The disparity between this side of the man, who is married and has two children, and his criminal record (most recently for assault), is partially explained, in Kroetz's understanding of it, by social inequities. He wanted to 'better' himself, but when he failed as an electronics gadget salesman he had too much pride to go back to work as a delivery man, and thus fell upon hard times. Kroetz has Schuster express his yearnings in a 'Song of Freedom' about a great model plane pilot whose craft will 'greet the sun'. Schuster fantasizes a personal revenge, in which he beats ten policemen single-handedly, but Kroetz, as he does with the other characters, relates this private anger to broader social and economic factors. His 'Song of Hope' catalogues luxury consumer items and has the refrain:

Buy, people buy!
That'll keep the rich man rich,
And the poor guy poor.

All three inmates sing parts of one song, 'On Reading Matter', in which they tell of the popular literature (romances, magazine pulp stories, detective novels) which they have available to them, and which they enjoy. The point Kroetz is making of course is that this sort of material is a sure means of preventing any basic change of consciousness among the lower orders of society.

For the Bochum premiere of *Lienz: City of the Dolomites*, directed by Istvan Bödy, designer Wolf Münzner created a large painted backdrop of a fairy tale Alpine scene, in front of which the barest essentials of a prison cell were placed for the actors to use. The 'fabulous' background and harshly real foreground aptly present the basic elements in Kroetz's play. The commentary and the contrasts are broad, while the human essence, the foreground, remains very real. It is in that foreground reality, as it were, that his strength as a playwright remains.

8
Voices from East Germany: Heiner Müller and Thomas Brasch

Like Franz Xaver Kroetz, Heiner Müller (b. 1929) is a confirmed Marxist, but his historical perspective derives from early experiences in Nazi and wartime Germany, followed by the construction period of the German Democratic Republic. Virtually all of his plays (there are over thirty) are concerned with aspects of this history, either in realistic modern East German settings, or in broad historical and mythic fashion, relating divided Germany's special 'misery' (to use Brecht's term) to traditions of Teutonic barbarism and Prussian authoritarianism, or to crucial moments in the twentieth century such as that following World War I, when Germany failed to create its own Marxist revolution. Müller's voice, unlike the voices of the most successful West German and Austrian dramatists, encompasses a wide range of experience and literature. The seriousness and importance of theme, coupled with the openly experimental attitude toward form, make him one of the more interesting of German language playwrights

117

currently receiving attention. Müller has 'quarried' the classics, as Brecht before him, adapting numerous works, including Brecht's. He has written under several names, and is an indefatigable reviser of his own early work. Precise chronology cannot be attached to many of his plays, since he usually works piecemeal. I will use the words 'early' and 'late' to refer to general trends in the form and content of his work. (Dates given are of the most recent versions.) It is significant for Müller, whose central theme is the idea of continuing revolution, that no work is ever completely finished.

Müller's first plays explore the immediate problems of reconstructing Germany on the socialist model. Residual Nazi consciousness among citizens, the gap between party rhetoric and daily reality, the burden of personal sacrifice needed to fulfil long-term utopian goals: these form the backbone of plays with titles like *Construction, Tractor, The Farmers.* Müller's commitment to socialism hasn't stopped short of criticism directed at governing régimes, a fact which has regularly caused him difficulty in having his plays performed in East Germany. A type who recurs in these plays and in the plays of other East German playwrights (*e.g.* Volker Braun) is the individual worker who finds it difficult to conform to state norms, though he usually overcomes his objections. One can see Müller, in his early work, as such a 'worker-writer', as it were, who had adjusted his plays in response to official and audience criticism.

The following passage from *The Scab* (1969) is typical of elements in the plays which caused him difficulty. Apparently, Müller's attitude toward the characters who were speaking was unimportant to his censors; the isolated speeches were objectionable:

GESCHKE: There's no socialism in America, but there are workers who drive their own cars. In socialism there's shoe rationing. Explain that to me.

SCHORN: The car belongs to the worker. But who owns the worker? We get our shoes on ration. But the auto factories are ours.

AN OLD WORKER: You can talk. But who is going to tell us that you're right.

In some of his plays, Müller has reworked classical materials in order to achieve an aesthetic distance (he refers to it as 'alienating the whole') while treating contemporary themes. The strategy is Brechtian. In *Philoctetes* (1966), Neoptolomus vacillates in sympathy for Philoctetes until stabbing him in the back to further the Greek cause. Müller exploits pure theatricality to set an 'alienated' tone at the start of the play. The actor playing Philoctetes delivers the first part of the prologue in a clown mask: 'What we show has no moral. You'll learn nothing from us about how to live your life.' He then strips the mask to reveal a death's head, before concluding the prologue: 'There's nothing to laugh at in what we're about to do with one another.' At the end of the play Neoptolomus carries Philoctetes' corpse from the stage, while Odysseus bears the weapon, the sacred bow, they had come to obtain. Müller remarks in a note that while they exit it would be possible 'to project pictures from the history of warfare, from the Trojan to the Japanese'. The idea of projections is only an explicit and obvious manifestation of Müller's use of the classics as a focus for the present. Sacred bows are never totally divorced from 'preventive' nuclear strikes in Müller's dramaturgy, nor is the ethical dilemma of twentieth-century revolutionary practice ever far from sight in the classic material.

119

Different in mode from the realistic plays and the classical adaptations is Müller's learning play *Mauser* (1970), written with another kind of classic, Brecht's *The Measures Taken*, clearly in mind. *Mauser* also parallels *Philoctetes* in some details, as the main character, referred to as A, faces a task the revolution has forced on him: to replace an inadequate executioner. The play presents the trial of A, who is shown grappling with the 'work' of revolution. Accepting the 'teachings' of the chorus, he does kill with machine-like coldness. But eventually he goes beyond the limits of his task, and kills with a passion, 'not for the revolution', an act condemned by the chorus. The A of Müller's play is one step beyond Brecht's main character in *The Measures Taken*. The first person to be executed in *Mauser* is in fact precisely the central Brecht character who had been judged guilty of 'premature humanity' for refusing to kill three farmers, unwitting 'traitors' of the revolution. A is asked to consider his 'job to be done' a piece of work 'like any other' in the revolutionary cause. In *Mauser*, Müller explores the reality of an ideology which, for the sake of humanity, can justify inhuman acts. Müller's tone is not judgmental, however: he presents the contradictions openly, as part of a dialectic.

'The daily bread of the revolution is the death of its enemies', says the Chorus in *Mauser*, and, 'Killing is a science which must be learned so it can be stamped out.' Müller presents such sentiments in a context which makes glib acceptance *or* dismissal of the idea impossible. Unlike Brecht, Müller depicts in *Mauser* conditions known to have existed in the building of a revolutionary Russian society. It is in that regard less abstract than Brecht's piece.

A's resistance to his role as executioner – 'every third one who faces my revolver [the 'Mauser' of the title] is possibly innocent' – is important to Müller, and forms a central theme of his plays. 'I am a human being. And human beings are not machines', cries A. When A accepts his own death at the end of the play, reaffirming his commitment to the revolution, he does so with the words of the Chorus, printed in the text in boldface: **Death to the Enemies of the Revolution.** The tone seems to be as contradictory as the whole piece: the Chorus's words, but uttered in fear and protest. For Müller, as for Brecht before him, the ethics of revolutionary practice are not clear and simple, and their full implications need to be explored openly.

Müller was asked what the function of theatre might be after the gap between audience and stage had been closed, and he replied in words which could apply to the necessary conditions for a proper reception and understanding of *Mauser* in a revolutionary or post-revolutionary society:

> Then the theatre has its very own function: namely that people can play through their own lives, and variations on situations. People who beforehand and afterward do something quite different. Then the theatre has its own function as a laboratory.[1]

'Playing through their own lives' for Müller and for citizens of his socialist society would include even the historical realities like revolutionary practice in Russia, removed in time but still significant in shaping revolutionary consciousness. The idea of a learning play in which the players themselves and their audiences, when not an interchangeable group, learn about the contradictions by dramatically engaging in them is close to Brecht's idea of a *Lehrstück*. Müller's *Mauser* differs from *The Measures Taken* in that it shows in explicit passionate scenes actual revolutionary practice based on historical reality.

In the play *Cement* (1972, based on a Soviet novel by Gladkow) Müller combines several of the themes from his earlier plays and, by inserting lengthy prose commentaries (passages on Achilles' voyage, the liberation of Prometheus, Herakles and the Hydra) spoken by different characters, expands his theatrical form. The classical commentaries allow him to express personal emotional responses to the complexities of revolution while retaining a formal distance.

The core of *Cement* consists of realistic scenes and scenes of high melodrama depicting the struggles, personal and social, faced by Russian revolutionaries in the period after the Civil War (1921) when the New Economic Policy signalled the beginning of a new bureaucratic order. Müller draws certain parallels between that situation and contemporary East Germany whose revolution, after all, was imported from Russia.

In one scene, the returning revolutionary hero Chumalov faces his class enemy Kleist, an engineer with the skills needed to build a new world: specifically here, the cement factory. He overcomes his desire for revenge and addresses Kleist in language reminiscent of twenties expressionism:

CHUMALOV: You don't know very much about yourself.
    Kleist, we will show you who you are.
    Your graveyard will become a monument
    To liberated labour when our new factory
    Rises from it, and other factories your head
    Cannot imagine, Kleist. Work is our heaven. . . .
    Take your skull in your hand. There is a new
    World to be built.

What follows is over sixty lines of commentary, which Müller suggests Chumalov deliver, on the liberation of Prometheus. The situation of Chumalov forcing Kleist into the new world is evoked poetically by Müller in the story of Herakles rescuing Prometheus. The passage begins: 'Prometheus brought lightning to humans, but did not teach them to use it against the Gods, because he shared his meals with the Gods, and they would have been less sumptuous if shared with humans.' A reluctant Prometheus ('Roaring and spitting with rage, he protected his chains from the grip of the liberator') eventually finds himself clinging to his liberator's neck, guiding him through wave after wave of arrows fired by the wrathful Gods. Müller concludes:

Meanwhile, screaming loudly to the heavens which were darkened by the swirl of stones, he declared his innocence in the liberation. The suicide of the Gods followed. One after the other they hurled themselves down from the heavens onto Herakles' back, and shattered in the rubble. Prometheus worked his way back onto the shoulders of his liberator and assumed the pose of the victor who rides on a sweating horse to meet the cheers of the populace.

The scene which follows, entitled 'The Administration or Christ The Tiger' shows Chumalov in a very prosaic argument with a new bureaucrat, Badyin: 'It's a disgrace, Comrade Chairman. Our dead aren't even buried yet, and you already act like generals, attacking the working class with typewriters. The bureaucracy.' Disparities between fixed notions of what revolutionary practice should mean and the thousand mundane tasks needed to effect lasting change have their parallel in private matters as well.

123

Chumalov fought in the revolution, but the assertive part of his nature which made him a hero there is seen as anachronistic when applied to his conventional relationship to women.

Chumalov dislikes Badyin for more than just professional or idealistic reasons, since he has learned that his wife Dasha had slept with Badyin while her husband was away at war. But Dasha is no longer sexual property. The changes brought by the revolution include a potentially new role for women, as equal partners in struggle. The new self-assured Dasha confronts her non-plussed husband early in the play with *her* new reality, and through the course of the action we learn of her sacrifices (sexual abuse, the placement of her child in an appallingly inadequate child care centre) and her confirmation of a hope in the new social and economic order. Some of the scenes are straight melodrama, as the following, in which Dasha is held captive by a 'white' officer and his cossack soldiers.

DASHA: I am still waiting for my death.
OFFICER: One must never keep a lady waiting.

He sets her free, and the stage directions read:

(*The Cossacks let go of the rope. Dasha stands unsteadily, with the noose loose around her neck, rubs her arms, tries to take steps, etc. Laughter from the Cossacks, the officer laughs too. The laughter stops abruptly, the officers and the Cossacks fall to the ground. The officer is dead immediately, the Cossacks move a few more times in slow convulsions, as if they were continuing to laugh silently, or looking for the most comfortable position for death. A moment of*

quiet. *Enter Red Army soldiers with rifles and Badyin
with a revolver. Badyin runs to Dasha. Dasha takes
the revolver out of his hand and empties the magazine
into the dead officer on the ground.*)

SOLDIER: He's dead already. Why did you shoot?
DASHA: (*to Badyin*) Before this noose I didn't want your
love. (*Slips the noose over his head.*) I want to sleep
with you, Comrade Badyin.

At the end of the play it is another woman who protests
against the compromising of revolutionary ideals in the
New Economic Policy. Polya tells Chumalov that 'Badyin
and others like him will destroy us./They'll be the hammer
of capitalism/which nails the revolution to the cross.'
According to Müller, Chumalov may even become a
Badyin in time, a compromiser and a bureaucrat. The last
line in the play, before the epilogue, is left to Polya, who
had ominously picked up a revolver at the sound of
Badyin's voice over a loudspeaker announcing in unctuous
rhetoric the successful opening of the new cement factory.
She had been expelled from the party, we learn, as she
speaks to the bumbling ex-bourgeois intellectual, Ivagin:

IVAGIN: We can't stop history the way we stop a horse,
just anywhere it pleases us. We won't make it within
humankind. But what is needed here is cement.
POLYA: You don't need to tell me where my place is.
(*Opens the window. Sirens.*)

Women's Comedy (1969, adapted from the radio play
Female Brigade, by his first wife, the late Inge Müller)
light-heartedly presents the same theme in a contemporary

setting. The play questions the extent to which legal assurances of sexual equality correspond to the facts under German socialism. A male character in the play states the theme of sexual inequity with cheerful sarcasm: 'Do you know this one? Capitalism is exploitation of mankind by mankind. Socialism is the exploitation of men by women.' Müller explores this basic sexual form of exploitation within varieties of revolutionary situations.

Müller's own mixed feelings about the painfully contradictory process of revolutionary transformation find expression in passages like the section in *Cement* entitled 'Herakles 2 or The Hydra'. Müller intends this piece to be spoken by the entire cast and to be 'made viable' by dramatic means: pantomime, script projections, sound. The prose commentary conveys a dizzying sense of confusion as Herakles, searching for the beast, discovers he is in fact inside the beast, that the gentle undulations he feels and his gradual envelopment by the 'dark forest' are the movements of a monstrous digestive system, 'reducing him again and again in steady destruction to his smallest components', out of which he repeatedly reconstructs himself – to the sound of the chorus in his ears – *'Keep within the bounds let off steam give up'*.

The imagery and tone are in places reminiscent of Beckett, a playwright Müller frequently cites as important to him. Once asked if Ionesco had influenced him, Müller explained that Beckett had had a greater effect, especially since he had begun to direct his own plays in Germany. 'I find it [*Waiting For Godot*] very radical and provocative.' Herakles considering his own present reality in *Cement* echoes any number of perplexed Beckett figures:

He also had the distinct feeling that his feet were becoming heavier. He counted the possibilities: (1) His feet were becoming heavier and the ground was sucking in his feet. (2) His feet felt heavier because the ground was sucking him in. (3) He had the impression that the ground was sucking in his feet because they were becoming heavier. These questions occupied him for a time. (years hours minutes). He found the answer in the increasing dizziness which the concentrically blowing wind caused in him: his feet were not becoming heavier, the ground was not sucking them in. One like the other was an illusion caused by his falling blood pressure. That calmed him and he walked faster. Or did he only believe that he was walking faster?

In Müller's later plays, this private agonizing element has grown in importance, to the point where the fragmentary scripts (which resemble his classical commentaries) rely less and less on a frame of plot or conventional character. The increasing emphasis on 'fragments for the theatre', as Müller sees it, relates to the current global situation, and to the intellectual's attempt to understand it. In the modern age, time speeds up, events multiply into complications beyond the individual's capacity to comprehend them, and his scripts offer possibilities for the theatre to communicate these facts and impressions in a form appropriate to them.

Müller once considered writing a play about a Hamlet figure in the days of the Hungarian rising in 1956, and though his fragmentary piece *Hamletmachine* (1977) is not actually about a specific historical situation, it does in its nine scant pages of text (no dialogue) present the private dilemma of the intellectual, like the author himself, in a contemporary world at the brink of annihilation – as Müller more and more tends to perceive the present situation. The theme of the individual struggling within historical and social matrices has found subjective expression in his most recent plays.

Müller has stated that it will be of increasing importance to the writer not to disengage himself from the work he produces: 'The idea of objectivity is totally empty'.[2] And though his work never approaches the 'new subjectivity' orientation of Handke (whom he admires) or others in the West, the recent trend in his work is an interesting parallel. His interest in Artaud is significant:

> Artaud tried to use his psychosis – or neurosis – as the point of departure in his theatre work. That, of course, was a disturbance of 'business as usual' in the theatre. This, it seems to me, is the function of today's playwright and theatre-person: to disturb the peace, the corruption, the habits, the comforts, *etc.* Today, the negative attitude is the positive one.[3]

Hamletmachine he describes as a 'self critique of the intellectual's position', and not unrelated to the sense of a failed revolution experienced by Western intellectuals since 1968: 'Hamlet in the play decapitates Marx, Lenin and Mao,' though Müller explains that is only one aspect of the play.

Müller chose to bring his most recent fragmentary piece to theatrical life himself, directing it with his wife, Ginka Tscholakowa. *The Mission – Memory of a Revolution* (*Der Auftrag – Erinnerung an eine Revolution*) (1980) was given its premiere in a forty-seat house allowing Müller, according to André Wirth who reviewed the play in *Theater heute*, to supply the audience with direct experience, as if they were 'not observing Antoine [a central figure] but simply sitting inside his head'.[4] The play as written, and the quality of production as described, has a definite neo-expressionist tone and intensity. Müller's stated aim to make history itself and its pressure on the individual psyche into a viscerally experienced reality in the theatre may well have succeeded under his own direction. At one point in the production, Jürgen Holz, who was cast in the central roles of both disappointed revolutionaries, opened a window in the theatre and shouted several lines about the 'yoke of freedom': his words could be heard to echo from the East German street below.

Inspiration for *The Mission* came from a story by the left-wing writer Anna Seghers, a refugee from Hitler, about the former bureaucrat of the French Revolution, Antoine, who fell into disapproval under Napoleon and who in the period of the Directorate issued papers to the three revolutionary Zealots – the heir to wealth in land and slaves, Debuisson; the Breton farmer, Galloudec; and the black, Sasportas – commissioning them to foment rebellion among the natives of the Antilles. In his play, Müller does not spell out details of plot, but rather presents the attitudes of hope, trust, betrayal and despair which eat their way into the psyches of the characters in the historical drama.

The Mission opens with the words of the dying Galloudec, in the form of a letter describing the demise of Sasportas on a Port Royal gibbet, and the retrenchment of Debuisson to the comforts of position. Their chief Antoine denies them, by renouncing a letter from Galloudec which returns the commission 'so others can carry on' with the work. He revels in his own masochistic memories of the French Revolution, while dousing himself ritually with wine: 'Look at my France. Breasts steeped in lye. A desert between her thighs.' His wife invites Antoine to bed, and the erotic imagery merges with the political. An 'Angel of Death', using Antoine's wife's voice, as in a dream, tells of

129

Debuisson, Sasportas, and Galloudec, who play their roles
– 'owner', 'slave', 'peasant' – to further the revolution. To
do so they turn a blind eye to the criminal mistreatment of
blacks, thereby denying their own humanity.

Debuisson's self-doubt parallels Antoine's though his
experience is presented more directly. To stress the point in
production Müller had the same actor play Debuisson and
Antoine. 'Maybe I really was waiting for this General
Bonaparte,' Debuisson says, 'Just as half of France waited
for him. Revolution is exhausting, Galloudec. The generals
arise in the sleep of the people and break the yoke of
freedom, so heavy to bear. Do you notice how your
shoulders stoop, Galloudec?' To the black, Sasportas,
France is irrelevant, the current necessity being revolution
in the Antilles. Debuisson's despair elicits a striking
gesture from Sasportas, who slashes his own hand and
smears Debuisson's face with the blood, exclaiming: 'The
home of the slave is rebellion'. In near-morality-play
fashion, Debuisson is described as being tempted by
treachery and virtually raped by happiness. The hope of
the slaves, of the third world (Africa, Asia) resides with
Galloudec and Sasportas, both doomed, while Debuisson
cries in despair: 'Don't leave me alone with my mask which
is already merging into my flesh and which no longer
causes me pain. Kill me before I betray you. I blanch at my
own shame, Sasportas, at being happy in this world.'

Reviewing Müller's production, André Wirth
catalogued the range of styles and motifs apparent in the
play derived from the modern repertory:

Müller's fertile groundwork Brecht, with variations
from Büchner (Antoine as Danton), Kafka (the search
for a mission), Genet (skin color as mask), Beckett (life
without a mission), Marcuse and Reich (eros and

politics), with unavoidable self-quotations: an impossible collage, which only Heiner Müller can bring off, and which grows into a unique theatre of cruelty à la Artaud.[5]

The difficulty and remoteness of Müller's work accounts for its being relatively little known or produced in English speaking countries, though the most recent fragments, which rely less on specifics of East German reality, may change that. Certainly in Germany his plays are seen as among the most challenging contemporary theatre pieces.

Thomas Brasch

The work of Thomas Brasch (a dozen plays, poetry, prose, and one film) draws its material from Germany's past in a mode similar to Müller's latest plays, though Brasch has been quick to point out that for him the central interest is in the lot of the individual, and that his experience of the German reconstruction period necessarily differs from that of the older Müller. For Brasch, the Berlin Wall as a central metaphor extends well beyond its political significance to include sexual and psychological barriers.

Brasch was born in England in 1945 of Jewish emigré parents, who settled after the war in East Germany where his father made a career with the governing SED party. Brasch himself fell foul of official circles several times before emigrating to the West in 1976; he was even incarcerated briefly for distributing leaflets in protest against the Soviet invasion of Czechoslovakia. Before restrictions on his work forced him to emigrate he had held various labouring and academic jobs. His one play to be performed in East Germany, written for production at a school and removed by censors after one performance, significantly dealt with the first victim of the Berlin Wall.

In a letter to Christof Nel, who directed the premiere of *Rotter* (1977) in Stuttgart, Brasch stressed that 'it is not primarily a play about history, Germany East and West, or similar material, but about the life of a particular man'. Notebook entries with the script of *Rotter* indicate a realist's interest in the details of everyday behaviour; observations garnered, as with Franz Xaver Kroetz, in the working environment. At the same time he bristles at the thought of aesthetic norms:

> What does it mean 'to make' the 'little' man a 'hero', to present the 'everyday'? As long as this process of art-consumption is locked up with the notion of the 'little man', it remains uninteresting. When Galileo can be recognized in your neighbour – then Brecht can be happy. For this reason attentiveness at the workplace is necessary.

Characters in Brasch's plays are not primarily understood in class terms, though historical conditions and real (usually crumbling) environments shape them. The loose episodic structure of his plays, and the penchant for startling visual images, indicate an interest in communicating aspects of life beyond the naturalist's range of observation.

Brasch explained that making the film *Iron Angel* (1981) allowed him to develop a purely visual means of communication which could speak directly to those inarticulate members of the audience whose lives parallel the figures in the film. In *Iron Angel* a seventeen-year-old legendary Al Capone character (based on a real person) teams up with a well-heeled bi-partisan executioner to

form a brief-lived underworld empire in the rubble of post-
World War Berlin, while the 'iron angels' of the title fly
their daily missions with Care packages into the
barracaded city. Brasch's vivid imagery in the film, and the
concrete post-war setting are natural developments from
his plays.

Lovely Rita (1978), a one-act play, also takes place in
post-war Berlin, and depicts the main character's physical
and psychological struggle for survival. In the process,
Rita murders her male 'Keeper', an officer of the
occupying forces, and betrays her female compatriots, and
thereby her sex as a whole. The action of *Lovely Rita* is
framed with images from or associated with movies: the
opening scene shows Rita, silent, apparently watching a
film, while from a loudspeaker we hear lines of dialogue.
Five women comment on Rita's behaviour as she watches:
'Now she thrusts steel through the skin, into the vein.' The
play closes with shots from an actual film: 'Rita on a toilet,
putting a coat hanger between her legs', and exclaiming, 'I
am all I need. I don't need a copy of myself, or even worse,
a copy of him. . . . I want to be alone.' The film is
evidently a screen test and preview for the occupation
censors, because an officer then comments to its director,
'If you insist on having this girl, we'll agree to it.'

One theme here is loss of identity; this loss is experienced
personally by Rita, but the play also broaches the question
of female identity and the identity of the German nation
itself after World War II. One of the women in *Lovely Rita*
cries out: 'You are like this country; raped without a
struggle, spreading your legs to strange thighs, strange
tongues, bearing worms that crawl until they fall into the
pit.' In striking theatre imagery, Brasch captures the
frustrations of his seventeen-year-old heroine trying to
understand herself. She delivers a pained monologue with

her head pressed against the horn of a car; and at another point gazes into a mirror:

> To speak. To speak words into the mirror. To let them become strange like words you once hear. To hold your face very close to the mirror and speak each letter very slowly onto the smooth surface until it clouds over with your breath and you can't recognize your face any more. Now to speak; my name is Rita. Your name is Rita. Our name is Rita.

Brasch explains that he wrote *Lovely Rita* as a way of coming to grips with his own personal situation, and that of his 'lost generation', as he describes his contemporaries who are not quite able to identify with the period of war-chaos, nor with the ideas of a future projected by either Germany. He stresses that when he criticizes East Germany he is using it as a model of any stagnant society. For Brasch from the East, the formalized repression of state 'order' elicits a similar response to that of Handke, ten years before, to any imposed system. An anarchy of temperament unites Brasch and such Western writers as Handke and Fassbinder.

Brasch's major full-length play, *Rotter, A German Fairy Tale* (1977), traces the dubious career of a 'little man', as he makes his way from Jew-baiter in 1932, to enthusiastic petty officer in the German army, to a loyal citizen (he turns people in for 'incorrect behaviour') and hero of labour in the German Democratic Republic of the mid-sixties. Rotter is the eternal time-server, ready to 'build the future' in blind obedience, changing his uniform as often as necessary to suit the political climate. He is no simple villain or fool, however, as Brasch presents him caught up by the movement of history, and the victim of private frustrations which make him susceptible to fascistic political machines. Misguided sexual energies, Brasch seems to be saying, distort Rotter's sense of life: he becomes a *perpetuum mobile* for any ideology to adapt to its purpose.

Rotter's nemesis in the symbolic struggle of the play is his friend Lackner, a man who abjures any public commitment, declaring 'I belong to me'. (Brasch's psychology is a bit oversimplified in that he also makes Lackner a successful 'ladies' man'.) When a general strike is in the air on 17 June 1953 in Berlin both Rotter and Lackner refuse to participate: the former as loyal citizen, the latter as fiercely independent individual.

In his preliminary notes to the play, Brasch makes it clear that he will need to employ formal techniques which transcend naturalism in order to capture the dislocated and frantic quality of Rotter's life. The play's subtitle, *A German Fairy Tale*, the use of doggerel verse, and such elements as two sinister clowns who disassemble Rotter's body and from it construct a huge puppet, or the two philosophers who examine psychological specimen Rotter, set the play apart from conventional naturalism. A gnomic band of 'old children' also functions as a chorus in the play, punctuating scenes with disturbing commentary and mime.

Christof Nel's premiere production stressed these aspects of the play from the start. In the first scene we see butcher's apprentice Rotter at work on the suspended carcass of a full grown swine ('Is there a small difference at least, between me and this dead common beast?'). With him in the scene are a customer, and Rotter's boss, unhappy at Rotter's incompetence. Nel had these two play the scene on stilts, and padded the bald master butcher to enormous proportions, also giving him a Hitler moustache and tiny lapel swastikas. The stage imagery, which complements Brasch's script, with its roots in popular fairground theatre, recalls Brecht's Weimar Republic production of his own *Man is Man*. Later in the scene, Rotter accidentally slits his own artery while at work on the swine's entrails. The 'old children', stanching the flow of his blood, declare: 'Before he plummets to the depths, our hero,/We'll quickly make of him an undisputed zero.' ('Aus diesem Mann soll werden erst ein Nichts/bevor er abtritt in *die Keller des Gerichts,*': literally, '*the cellar of the law*'). Rotter's light-headedness, presumably caused by the loss of blood, can partially account for the vision of the 'old children' here, but the internal/external axis of the play is basic to Brasch's dramaturgy. The technique is reminiscent of proto-expressionist pieces by Strindberg, where the boundaries between internal and external reality become blurred. The autopsy by two strange philosophers, one of whom finds Rotter to be a 'blank piece of paper' for history to write on, also parallels Ibsen's *Peer Gynt*, in the fantastic madhouse scene. Brasch writes in his working diary of a possible staging, clearly referring to expressionist technique: a massive head (Rotter's) set upstage, out of which leap the figures in the various scenes, and into which they return at the end of the play.

Brasch gives his play two sequential conclusions, in fulfilment of the challenge Rotter had hurled at Lackner at the end of the first scene: 'Your life against mine.' Directly after Rotter's agonizing 'death dream' with the two clowns and the pair of philosophers described above, Rotter and Lackner, now minus an eye from a war wound, are discovered in a deep tunnel. In part one, they struggle over Rotter's heart medicine (Lackner quips 'I didn't know you had a heart') before Rotter clubs Lackner to death. His dying words are: 'Three years of my life are better than your fifty years dying.' Rotter then puts his ear to Lackner's breast while the heartbeat fades. His antagonist dead, he casts away his heart medicine and the scene ends.

In part 2, the 'old children' and the ghosts of three soldiers betrayed and abandoned by Rotter during the war are also present. This time Lackner administers the medicine to Rotter, but the 'old children' laugh and go berserk, chasing Lackner from the stage. The dead men demand Rotter become their 'leader' (*Führer*), and, with the words 'We'll start all over again', he leads the grotesque march of ghosts and wicked ageless dwarfs into 'the tunnel, the emptiness'.

Either way, Brasch seems to be saying, Rotter is the one who survives. With Lackner dead, heartlessness triumphs, but it is shown to be isolated: the ironic 'embrace' while Rotter listens for the last pulse beat reinforces this. In the second version, Lackner is merely banished, but his humanity (giving Rotter the medicine) has ironically enabled the fascist monstrosity to march again. Brasch's purpose is the suggestiveness of a Grimm Fairy Tale, not the resolution of a clear plot line. The double ending preserves ambiguity.

The imagery of Brasch's *Iron Angel*, as described in *Der Spiegel* (27 April 1981) indicates the continuing lyrical and suggestive thrust of Brasch's imagination:

Children playing among the throngs of black-marketeers; a dead dog in the gutter; a covey of young girls in white summer dresses next to a blind hurdy gurdy player [played by Brasch himself]; rickety prams as preferred transport for contraband; the flaming wreck of an aircraft in the process of being looted; a tiny blond Berliner who dances meticulously with a tall negro WAC; war widows at a seance; a broken down truck

137

drawn by an old nag; a van mounted with a loudspeaker which floods the eery abandoned streets with Italian opera; . . .

An interviewer suggested that Brasch's work betrays a mixture of anarchism and bitterness. The playwright's response to this gives an idea of his current state of mind and the attitude expressed in his work:

I'm not bitter. I just have the feeling that what's constantly being talked about has nothing to do with me. At the moment I'm probably in most sympathy with someone who stands up against the wall of his house and watches the traffic go by, and with a certain cheerfulness asks: how much longer can it really go on like this? Nothing's quite right anymore.

(*Die Zeit*, 8 May 1981)

9
Private Visions:
Thomas Bernhard
and Botho Strauss

I had a friend I used to drink a glass of wine with, a thoroughly petty bourgeois type, who wrote darling little poems and wretched prose and was stupid, the way petty bourgeois types are, and he had had three wives and with each one, two children, and he felt right pleased with himself there with his pot belly and shopkeeper's smock, and he went home one day and dressed up in his wife's Dirndl and padded his breasts and hanged himself in the doorframe in this outfit, a man about forty five years old who gave no hint that he was fed up with his life.[1]

After Bernhard told this anecdote, his interviewer asked whether he would agree that a 'moment of comedy' could have saved the friend had he chanced to glimpse himself in a mirror before the critical final second. 'Actually, yes', Bernhard answered, though he was quick to explain that in principle he disapproved of interfering with any man's right to suicide. The mordant humour and satirist's eye for grotesque detail in this little story are characteristic features of Bernhard's work, as is the attitude in the response to the question: any effect his work might have on individuals beside himself is purely incidental to the writer's purpose. Asked on another occasion (*Der Spiegel*, 23 June 1980) whether he wrote about such things as suicide to keep from hanging *himself*, he answered: 'Could be, yes, sure.'

The nearest one could come to categorizing Bernhard would be as a bitter and austere writer within the tradition of the absurd. His vision is solitary and uncomfortable; his relative success with theatre audiences in Germany may attest both to the middle class German's penchant for self-criticism to the point of self-hatred, as Thomas Mann once put it, and perhaps, as Handke quipped in the late sixties, to the latent masochism of the theatre-going public. The images in the social mirror Bernhard offers his public are among the most severe to be found on today's German language stage.

Thomas Bernhard (b. 1931), two years younger than Heiner Müller, had his early schooling during the Nazi years in a Catholic seminary (he has said he hardly noticed the difference when the Nazis left) and drew from his experience of the war era his general conclusions about the capacity for society, and mankind, to destroy itself. There is no equivalent in Bernhard's thinking to Müller's faith in the force of revolutionary change, or any other kind of progress. Bernhard relentlessly meditates on intellectual torpor, physical deterioration and death; his vision is sharply misanthropic. He has written 'In the dark everything becomes clear', and it is into that dark side of his own mind that he invites readers and audiences.

He has expressed admiration for the sheer hopeless idealism of his communist uncle and socialist grandfather, but the object of their utopian longings left no strong

140

imprint on him. (Salary, and not ideology, is apparently what led him to work briefly as a reporter for a socialist newspaper.) Liberation is possible only in the imagination and for the individual. Implicitly, only the practice of art gives value to life, and given the number of plays in which either despairing or failed and ridiculous artists have prominent parts (*The Ignoramus and The Madman*; *The Force of Habit*; *Minetti*; *The Famous Ones*) even here Bernhard's vision is bleak. The absurd chasm between man's perception of his capabilities and reality is a constant theme of his work.

In his semi-autobiographical novel *The Cellar – A Withdrawal* (1976; 'semi' in that he refuses to classify and separate details of his 'imaginative' and 'real' lives in the fictions he has created out of his experience) Bernhard describes his grandfather in the post-war years:

> Day after day, I know, he'd lock himself in, and his wife, my grandmother, waited for the shot from the pistol he'd lain on the desk, at night under his pillow, she feared this shot, he had threatened all of us, again and again, he had no money and not the least bit of strength, starved like the rest of us, he knew now, two years after the war had ended, in the bitterest of times once again, nothing more than hopelessness.

The style of the passage is typical of Bernhard's work: a possessed mind in a rush of thought, which proceeds through contradictions and conflicting emotions as if by the inertia of its own forward motion. Several pages further in the novel the old man takes up his daily task, at 3 a.m., 'his struggle with the impossible, with the total hopelessness of writing'. For many of Bernhard's characters, as for himself, the last words of Beckett's *The*

Unnamable are appropriate: 'You must go on, I can't go on, I'll go on.'

Bernhard has kept writing, quite prolifically; since the success of his first major novel, *Frost* (1963), which depicts a man's psychological deterioration, he has produced a dozen plays (the first full-length play, *A Feast for Boris*, had its premiere in 1970), seven novels, numerous short stories, and some poetry. His fiction makes frequent conventional reference to the theatre as a metaphor – 'Nature is theatre as such [people are] actors from whom nothing much more is to be expected' (*The Cellar*) – and it seems only natural that he, as Beckett and others before him, would use the stage as a means to explore consciousness, and in his case to assault the audience.

The situations in Bernhard's first two plays are typical of his work. In *A Feast For Boris* a birthday party is thrown by a wealthy crippled woman ('The Good One') for her deformed, legless husband Boris; in the final torment, witnessed by thirteen fellow cripples and objects of the 'Good One's' charity, he is given a present of boots and long underwear. In *The Ignoramus and The Madman* (1972) an opera singer and surgeon are juxtaposed as two absurd 'specialists': the doctor talks incessantly about the details of autopsy, while the soprano prepares for a performance as the *Queen of Night* in The Magic Flute. Her drunken father listens to the doctor through much of the play, which ends with the daughter coughing spastically while she cancels further engagements. In virtually all of Bernhard's plays normal human values are turned inside out: philanthropy is sadism in *A Feast For Boris* while unique skill and beauty are fatuous narrow mindedness and affectation in *The Ignoramus and The Madman*. Positions of power, whether in personal or social terms, are always seen as loathsome.

142

More than one critic has noted the misanthropy of this author as having a special Austrian cast to it – shaped in part, it would seem, from the self imposed isolation of his remote mountain village where Bernhard, like numerous characters he has invented, resides. One thinks of reclusive characters in Adalbert Stifter's fiction – also a favourite of Handke's – in this context.

Among his contemporaries, Bernhard bears comparison with the younger Austrian Handke. Both authors' works derive in part from the Austrian stage tradition of dark humour and bitter satire in the nineteenth-century playwrights Nestroy and Raimund – the latter of whom, like Adalbert Stifter, took his own life. Linguistic patterns and repetition with variations are important structural features of both Bernhard's and Handke's plays, though Bernhard shows less interest in formal experiment in each work.

The musicality of the virtually unpunctuated long speeches in his plays may derive from Bernhard's early training in music, and its dependence on the specifics of the German language may explain why his plays have not enjoyed great success in translation. The resounding failure of *The Force of Habit* at the National Theatre in London in 1976 seemed inevitable. Benedict Nightingale in *The New Statesman* (19 November 1976) summed up the problem with the play, which depicts a ragged circus troupe's hopeless efforts to rehearse to perfection Schubert's *Trout Quintet*, conducted by their obsessed director:

A play like *The Force of Habit* proves nothing: it simply teases us with bizarre and foreign images which we're invited to translate into speculative statements about life. Bernhard's idea of gratifying a thirst is to fill the water-bottle with sand or, more accurately sound. He has somehow persuaded himself that drama is music, words crotchets and quavers.

Bernhard's attitude toward language and com-munication (and his interest in Wittgenstein) overlaps with Handke's, as does his idea of the artist in society. Both playwrights are clearly in the romantic tradition which sees the artist as isolated and writing for his own sake, out of private need. Bernhard's contempt for the idea that the writer can effect any but personal changes even goes further than Handke. One could take the statement in *The Cellar* as typical: 'I speak a language which only I understand, no one else, just the way everyone understands his own language, and those who think they've understood, they're idiots and charlatans.' While he considers actors totally ignorant about his writing, he carries the idea to an extreme when he concludes that neither could he explain or interpret his own work: he just does it, by compulsion.

Bernhard leaves his texts unpunctuated so that the reader or actor can find his own suitable tempo or rhythm: the dramatic scripts are, to use his own word, 'skeletons', to be fleshed in by others. One actor who has played the lead in a number of Bernhard premieres (the author carefully restricts the rights of his plays for particular directors and actors) is Bernhard Minetti. In a piece actually titled *Minetti* (1976), about an ageing actor waiting to be interviewed for *Lear*, the producer never shows up, and the final image of the play is Minetti sitting on a park bench while snow gradually blankets his body. In an interview by Claus Peymann (the director with whom he frequently collaborates on Bernhard scripts) Minetti described the typical situations in the plays as balanced between comedy and tragedy, and the typical characters as Hamlet-like, because they think aloud but do very little. Bernhard's extremely long speeches are especially challenging to an actor, according to Minetti. He must determine the movements of the character's consciousness from the outline Bernhard provides; choices must be made as to which spoken words are merely private reflection, which are less controlled emotional outbursts, and finally, which are uttered for the sole purpose of evoking responses from others on stage. Like Shakespeare's, Bernhard's plays are virtually devoid of 'stage directions'.

When I saw the premiere performance of *The World Reformer* (1980, Bochum, directed by Claus Peymann) Minetti's acting itself seemed part of Bernhard's total concept. One might call it 'ironic' acting, in keeping with one of the playwright's chief literary resources. *The World Reformer* presents, in two parts, the portrait of a misanthrope, a crotchety philosopher, nearly seventy years old, upon whom the academic worthies of Frankfurt University are about to bestow an honorary degree. (In *Immanuel Kant* [1978] Bernhard has the philosopher, his servant, and his parrot travel to New York University under the delusion that he is to receive a similar award: he is greeted by men in white coats.) The world reformer lives with an elderly concubine, whom he mistreats: at one point in the Bochum performance she tightened the knot on his tie while he gazed into her eyes, mocking her to take revenge in the very act of serving him: 'if only you knew how to tighten it – it makes you hateable – you wait'. After accepting the Frankfurt degree, he peremptorily orders the entire visiting party (including the mayor and vice-chancellor) out of his house. The self-mockery of the world reformer parallels the self-mockery of Bernhard the 'writer'. Minetti in the Bochum production, rolling his eyes after lines like the following, actualized the thought in performance:

> All roads unavoidably lead
> to perversity
> and absurdity.
> We can only improve the world
> if we destroy it [rolled eyes]
> Or do you think they understood my tractatus. [quizzical]

The acting itself transcends the banality of despair in the text.

The difficulty with Bernhard's plays is that they do not contain the range of possibilities of the classics of absurdist theatre. They are similar in theme to Beckett plays and have such features in common as images of crippled humanity or petty daily frustrations expressed through standard comic business (shoelaces that keep coming undone, hats that will not stay on), but they lack breadth of vision, or liberating humour. A Beckett prop usually has several levels of significance; for Bernhard such things are often flat and simple.

The cultured premiere audience at *The World Reformer* was certainly responding as much, or more to the performer as to the play, when Minetti rambled through a catalogue of remarks debunking the idea of culture and cultural institutions. (An additional irony for the German audience, Bernhard Minetti is a living cultural institution. His work dates back to the heyday of Weimar Republic theatre when he worked with such greats as Jessner.) Bernhard's mockery extends to the cultural ritual of attendance at highly subsidized world premieres. The Bochum audience laughed heartily at itself in Minetti's rambling monologue:

Private Visions: Thomas Bernhard and Botho Strauss

Would you like to go to Interlaken
A voice in me says
Yes
Another says no
Yes the one
Yes to Interlaken the one
No not to Interlaken the other
There's nothing I hate more than Switzerland
and nothing I hate more than nature
Let's think it over
Perhaps there's somewhere else
where we can spend a couple of happy days
Can't it be in the North
What do you have against the North
You always want to go South
That's a bit of sentimental weakness
In the high North the head stays clear
in the South it all goes weak and rotten
It's a perverse habit
to travel South
to seek out history
to dig up culture
I have always hated the so-called educational journies
I hate museums
the whole South
is one great big museum
Rome, what a horror my child
Sicily a fallacy
Athens a nightmare
From pillar to pillar
From grave to grave
From church to church
From Madonna to Madonna
I've always hated it

But I hate Interlaken even more
Get Interlaken right out of your head

At this point Minetti removed a cool cloth his common-law wife had placed on his head, claiming it no longer helped. At other moments of the performance he wore a wig, and a partially knitted wool cap – the needles still projecting from it obviously suggesting a mock crown of thorns.

Bernhard constructs his plays around such monologues, and shows disregard for realistic dramatic construction. When Handke toys with dramatic convention it is usually for a purpose, and he often displays a surrealist's sense of humour: wanting to underscore a 'meaningful event' in *They Are Dying Out* Handke calls for a garbage can lid to be thrown to the floor backstage. Bernhard's contempt for 'meaning' and for normal dramatic practice is expressed more nakedly. To clear the stage for a soliloquy in *The World Reformer* Bernhard has a phone ring from the wings, wastes no words on plausibility or rationalization in terms of plot, and off goes the extraneous character.

A recent play, *Before Retirement* (1979), offers insight into how facets of German history and social reality achieve dramatic form in Bernhard's work in comparison to that of his contemporaries. Georg Hensel described this 'comedy of the German soul' as his most elegant play: 'three performers, animated with Strindberg psychology, in a mythical situation, bedecked with Nazi emblems and packed with relevant political material.'[2] Rudolf Höller, a former deputy commandant of a concentration camp, and currently a high ranking official of the West German judiciary, lives with his two sisters. Clara, crippled by an American bomb blast in the last days of World War II, has left-wing sympathies, and loathes her brother, while Vera clings adoringly (and incestuously) to him. Höller has traditionally celebrated Himmler's birthday, but on this October 7th his guests have deserted him, so he puts on his SS uniform, drinks himself into a stupor, and threatens to shoot Clara. He collapses from a heart attack, Vera puts on a recording of Beethoven's Fifth Symphony (Höller had earlier said 'Music makes it all bearable') before welcoming the Jewish doctor; her bitter ironic penultimate lines accuse Clara: 'You're guilty/with your silence/you with your eternal silence.'

The thematic material of the play could be the substance of any number of post-World War II German plays; but whereas someone like Heiner Müller forces the audience to face the brutalities of German history and its continuing present influence, Bernhard's satirical thrust leads to a general misanthropy. The grotesque details of Höller's birthday party – reminiscing on Himmler's humanitarian act of saving Höller's life; leafing through a photo album which juxtaposes the trivial (holiday snaps) and the horrid (snaps of condemned Hungarian Jews); the 'demon's' love of music; the endless intoning of 'good German' clichés about duty and hard work – are not so much exposés, as they are illustrations of Bernhard's world view. While in the late seventies the issue of ex-Nazis in high-ranking West German government positions was a real one, Bernhard sees both the fact of reinstated Nazis and the idea of effectively changing things by exposing them as equally absurd. He has explained (*Der Spiegel*, 23 June 1980) that such people as these 'are in me, just as they are in everyone else.'[3] Even the idea of environmental protection, a topical subject in the seventies, finds its way into Bernhard's play: Höller draws strength from the conviction that his hero, Himmler, was also concerned with the environment. 'If Himmler hadn't lived/right where our house stands/ there would have stood a poison gas factory.' Himmler had rescued Höller, and now Höller fights to preserve the natural landscape (and would like to rid it of Jews and Americans, too). The satire is aimed at *homo sapiens*, rather than at any particular ruling group; there is no point in exposing corruption; it is as ubiquitous as it is amorphous.

In Franz Xaver Kroetz's play *The Nest* a working class character learns he has been unknowingly poisoning a lake at the bidding of his boss (and for extra pay); the results are nearly tragic. But something is learned about pollution and responsibility, and a change of consciousness results. No wonder that Kroetz, who once shared a literary prize with Bernhard, expresses contempt for the Austrian's work. The two represent opposite directions in contemporary German theatre. Bernhard's work is *sui generis*, both part of and aloof from the contemporary scene.

Botho Strauss

Botho Strauss (b. 1944) established himself as a critic for *Theater heute* and collaborated as a dramaturg with Peter Stein on, among others, the acclaimed productions of *Peer Gynt* (1971) and *Summerfolk* (1972) at the Schaübuhne am Halleschen Ufer before turning his full attention to fiction and playwriting. Strauss's direct experience of the theatrical process parallels several other writers considered in this book. Kroetz directs and acts in several media, frequently taking the opportunity to revise his own plays while staging them, Müller has similarly reshaped his plays as a director. Though Strauss has not worked extensively on productions of his own plays, his experience as Peter Stein's collaborator has left its mark on him. A good introduction to Strauss's play *Trilogy of Reunions*, to cite one example, would be to watch the filmed version of the Schaubühne production of Gorky's *Summerfolk* (1972). Strauss's play calls for a flow of movement perfectly illustrated by the Gorky play as done in Berlin.

The content and style of Strauss's plays share tendencies with Handke and Bernhard. The consciously 'poetical' and personal quality of his work, an absorption with the contours of language and the process of writing, and a similarity of themes link his plays to Handke's later efforts, though they are less consistently experimental in form. Like Bernhard and Handke Strauss abjures party political thinking, though he is sharply satirical of contemporary Germany: ' . . . a society like ours [in which] the ability of people to enjoy and to suffer appears to have shriveled more and more.' (*Trilogy of Reunions.*) The characters in his four full length plays are typically well-spoken and sensitive, variously gripped by neuroses, and aware both of the inadequacy of their emotional lives and of their inability either to express their true feelings or to do much to improve their situations.

Critics have associated Strauss with the 'new subjectivity' and the larger German Romantic tradition. Helmut Schödel says that Strauss echoes Clemens Brentano and Hugo von Hofmannsthal when he bemoans his failure (directly and through his characters) to articulate his thoughts and feelings.[4] Furthermore, once having uttered the sentences, he perceives them as objects alien to himself. 'Nowhere in the world,' Schödel quotes Strauss, 'have I come across anything stranger to me than a verbal expression which I myself have created.' Strauss's drama is peopled with characters out of touch with the world around them, with each other, ultimately with their inner selves. This problem finds concise expression at the conclusion of Strauss's novel *Devotion* (1977). The hapless writer/hero Robert Schroubeck is near despair of ever being reconciled with his lover. He types the words 'I haven't quite reached my goal yet . . .', crosses them out, and switches on the television where he recognizes an aged Hit Parade star apparently singing one of his formerly successful tunes.

> The artist, dragged in out of the past, no longer had the practised knack or, at this particular moment, the memory needed to move his lips convincingly in synchronization with the [scratched] record. The camera dared to move in for a close-up just once, but instantly beat a retreat. For while memory still sang in expansive tones, the old man's mouth suddenly shrivelled and twitched, mumbling a curse at having forgotten the text.

The melancholy and humour in this scene of displacement is typical of Strauss's work. Like Handke, his attitude toward his own romantic inclinations is ambiguous. While he suggests that the idea of an artist (here jokingly a 'pop' artist) is anachronistic, 'dragged in from the past', he values the ability to create something out of one's neurotic preoccupations.

In Strauss's first play, significantly titled *The Hypochondriacs* (1972), the idea of creating alternative subjective realities is central. In fact, as the play wears on the plot dissolves giving the impression that the main character, a writer named Vladimir, has conjured a substantial part of the action out of his imagination. Vladimir talks at length to other characters about dreams and tricks of perception, and about his own mental and emotional tangles. In the first act while he is talking in his sleep about his father, his paramour Nelly tells the servant that 'Sometimes Vladimir's fantasy leaps straight out of his brain and takes complete possession of him.' Though the tone of Strauss's play is distinctly lighter, there is a resemblance here to some of Thomas Bernhard's obsessed, tortured characters whose imaginations seem to control them instead of vice versa.

Set in Amsterdam in 1901, *The Hypochondriacs* has a broadly farcical romantic mystery story at its core. Mysterious figures appear, including a double of Vladimir forty years his senior who looks 'very very much' like him; gunshots shatter a large fishtank, then fell Vladimir's mother Elizabeth; a pair of sinister brothers, partners in a pharmaceutical concern, the one long and tall the other short and squat, embroil the main characters in industrial espionage and murder. In the third act the freudian burlesque involving Vladimir, his mother, and his lover reaches a critical point. Nelly threatens Vladimir's mother Elizabeth with a revolver. In comes Jakob, Vladimir's father (who may really be Vladimir in disguise) apparently to save his 'wife' Elizabeth; instead, he shoots her. When Nelly turns the gun on Jakob the empty chamber clicks and Jakob wheezes for breath. At the end of the play Jakob (Vladimir?) tells Nelly that he had masterminded the entire plot only to gain her favour. Then he stabs her to death and escapes with the servant Vera! There are very funny moments amidst all this confusion, and Strauss occasionally achieves effects akin to Strindberg's potent psychological shenanigans in a play like *Dance of Death*. *The Hypochondriacs* explores the border between sanity and madness, and the problem of shifting identity, themes which recur in all his work. The play, nevertheless, seems overwritten, especially in those parts where Strauss has Vladimir display his professional activity as a writer in long essayistic observations. The premiere of *The Hypochondriacs* lasted a full three hours on stage, an experience which drew boos from those of the audience who endured to the end. When Peter Stein directed the second major production of the play he accentuated the comedy and lightened the action with more satisfactory results.

Familiar Faces, Mixed Feelings (1975), Strauss's second play, is set in contemporary Germany and focuses on a group of characters from the real world in contrast to the detective fiction world of *The Hypochondriacs*. In this comedy, Strauss first naturalistically explores the mysteries of human, primarily romantic, relationships, then introduces a fantastical element in the person of a stage magician as a means of extending the author's ideas beyond the limitations of naturalistic conventions.

Familiar Faces takes place in a hotel in Königswinter, where seven friends have assembled for the Christmas season. They talk to and about each other mostly, and though their emotional lives have been and are intertwined we are never given a clear picture of precisely how they relate to one another. Individual motivations and exact relationships are unknowable for Strauss. As in Pinter's *Old Times* the reality of particular felt moments far outweighs in importance the verifiable facts of people's past lives together. Stefan owns the hotel. His wife Doris has an attachment to Guenther, who is the hotel servant and her partner in amateur dance competitions. When Stefan threatens to sell the hotel because he needs 'to change his life' thereby endangering the group's coherence, Guenther objects heartily in the arch style of dialogue: 'You'd really dare to put this highly sensitive communal group out on the street?!' There is something artifical, brittle, even absurd about the web of relationships in the play.

Well into the action a magician named Karl casts a spell

which allows a temporary harmony to reign for the group, a technique reminiscent of Handke's 'magician' Von Stroheim in *The Ride Across Lake Constance*. Strauss shares Handke's wistful yearning for such harmony, as well as his despair that it can ever be achieved. Thanks to magic in *Familiar Faces* sources of frustration and animosity are briefly suspended. The hotel will not be sold after all; out of nowhere, a 'double' of Doris appears who dances a perfect duet for once with Guenther; the impotent Stefan makes love to his wife. Strauss abruptly wrenches the play back from this pleasant fantasy in a final scene. Guenther has apparently frozen to death in the cold storage room, and his stiff body rests downstage with penis exposed to the others. The characters treat the matter indifferently – 'Leave it, he'll thaw out again' – and the play ends to a quick foxtrot tempo. With Stefan out of the way the group will survive to indulge their emotions and analyse their relationships another day. Human sympathy seems a thing of the past.

In *Trilogy of Reunions* (1976) Strauss created another closed society, an art group depicted as they spend a day in a gallery prior to the opening of a new exhibition entitled 'Capitalist Realism'. The pathos of unfulfilled relationships is still a central concern, though Strauss's choice of form in this play leaves behind the theatrical sleight of hand and 'magic' of his first two efforts. While working on the play Strauss described *Trilogy* as having 'lots of people who cross and disappear virtually before one has noticed them, everything [happens] just in passing. . .'. Though considerably longer (a four-and-a half-hour premiere) and more diffuse, *Trilogy of Reunions* bears a family resemblance to a Chekhov play in theme and technique; we are given glimpses of relationships and we notice an aimlessness and loss among Strauss's highly articulate people. 'We live from one separation to the next,' the writer Peter says. And the lead female Susanne confides to a rival her 'only hope' in making contact with the group's director Moritz: '. . . the same repetitive course . . . In the beginning always the separation . . . then comes a reunion . . . Between coming and going is the turning point, that's where we meet each other.' Susanne is forty two years old, desperately, sometimes viciously, fighting for her right to these 'turning points' as small consolations in her life.

Strauss orders the 'comings and goings' in such a way as to give an impression of interconnected tableaux, brief framed moments in the lives of the seventeen characters on one particular day. At the end of each scene, the stage goes black; with the return of light, changes in the groupings are revealed. The effect can be very stylized, as occurs the first time Kiepert, an ominous member of the board of directors, appears on stage. His name is invoked at the end of a scene. The lights switch off, then on again to reveal a man upstage, back to the audience, holding a child by the hand. Also silently present are his former wife at one end of the stage and the rest of the characters bunched together opposite her. They all contemplate Kiepert as he contemplates a painting on the back wall. Kiepert's power over the group is thus arranged and presented visually, as in a painting or photograph. In the Stuttgart premiere after each scene of the entire play large black 'shutters' appeared above and below the stage to meet at mid point and signal the change of scene.

Plot in *Trilogy of Reunions* has little relevance. The one crisis occurs when Kiepert censors the exhibition for displaying a painting he finds insulting, 'Carnival of Directors'; the removal of the piece clearly demonstrates where power resides. At the end of the play the curator of

156

the show Moritz says goodbye to Susanne, hangs 'Carnival of Directors' around his own neck and leans against the gallery wall. These are 'silly people', as one character refers to them, on display along with the pictures in their gallery. The more astute are painfully aware of this. There is a tendency in Strauss's work to place human emotions at a distance, to consider the characters as objects of study. During a slide presentation in the later play *Big and Little* we see a huge projection of an apple. The humorous commentary has a surrealist ring to it, and could apply to the people on stage in Strauss's plays as well as to the blow-up of an apple: 'Here you see an object that has gone far. / It is a symbol. Almost more a symbol than an object.'

The self-consciousness Strauss attributes to his characters borders at times on parody. They speak at length about their feelings, about art, about the state of the nation or the last novel they have read as if, like the author Strauss they had had their training writing critical reviews. It is plausible enough for actors to be demonstrative emotionally, but Strauss strains things when he has the young actor Answald whine to his father (also an actor) in disappointment and confusion over a broken love affair: 'She doesn't want me, she doesn't want to leave me. It's all so eternally unclear . . .' During another conversation a character begins to sneeze uncontrollably, explaining that all he needs to do is see a field of hay in a painting to set him going. 'Imagination maybe', he remarks, 'But the effect is the same.' The equivalent is true for Strauss's emotionally high strung characters, who often play at their feelings and fall victim to overactive imaginations, but who do seem to suffer as a result. The only real passion in *Trilogy of Reunions* is the director Moritz's for the art works in the gallery; one painting by Lucien Freud in particular rouses him as it transcends the banal in the act

157

of depicting it. The painting is preferable to the 'dwarfed emotions' of the mass of humanity in contemporary Europe. Implicitly Strauss seems to be engaged in the same activity as a playwright, making an art object out of paltry human substance.

A recent play, *Big and Little* (1978) is Strauss's most successful to date. The interest again is in shifting psychological and emotional states, but this time the focus is on one person, a lonely woman named Lotte (former physical therapist and graphic artist) as she tries desperately to make contact with people – both strangers and figures from her past such as an old school friend, her brother, and an estranged husband. In *Trilogy of Reunions* one of the most damning comments about a person is that 'in your heart you are ice and ashes'; there is something distinctly 'ice and ashes' about the emotional tone of Strauss's first three plays. In the cold social landscape of *Big and Little*, however, the figure of Lotte shows compassion for people around her and evokes a sympathy from the audience. Much of the play consists of Lotte talking to her most consistently attentive listener, herself. In the first scene she is on an Algerian holiday tour and eavesdrops on two unseen men hoping against hope that they will make a pass at her; in the tenth and final scene she blurts out details from her personal life to the embarrassed silence of a group of strangers in a physician's waiting room. Lines from the first scene – ' . . . nothing's right./Time passes, but not the way it should' – prove to have a pathetic and true ring to them by the last moments of the play, as Lotte sits alone and forgotten in the doctor's antechamber, having spent the night there.

The theme of alienation and isolation tie the scenic images together: eavesdropping on several occasions; Lotte poking her head into a strange couple's window to offer succour to an unhappy wife; Lotte and her television in an expressionistically 'gigantic' room in an apartment house. The world seems too much for the innocent Lotte; she greets each strange occurrence with astonishment and wonder. And strange they are! An abandoned seventeen year old she tries to talk to has 'had a taste of life' and since that time spends her days in a close-fitting pup tent. Lotte will eventually move into a telephone booth herself to live, complete with rubber tree, makeshift curtains, flypaper and a picture of her husband. The images of alienation are graphic.

Lotte's isolation is emblematic of a widespread condition. Designer Karl Ernst Hermann's rooming-house set in the Berlin premiere of *Big and Little* consisted of two rows of four brightly lit white rooms stacked one atop the other. Using light to focus attention on one or more of the rooms at a time, Hermann simply and clearly extended the metaphor of people locked in the separate cubicles of their lives. Strauss peoples the rooms of his apartment house with representative types from contemporary Germany. A guitar-playing crystallographer remarks on the state of physics – 'a little prison yard full of experts, walking around restlessly and pushing against the dark walls of the silence of the masses' – and later directly applies the image of isolation to the tenants surrounding Lotte: 'In theory, every room here is responsible for itself./That's a kind of silent house rule.' In her small way Lotte tries to be an exception to that rule. And Strauss successfully imbues her with a compassionate quality, as if there were truth in her claim to be one of the chosen thirty-six good people in the world promised by God to prop up each generation of mankind.

To emphasize Lotte's break from the microcosm her apartment house represents and from the world as a whole,

159

director Niels-Peter Rudolf (Bochum 1980) had her leave the stage (the waiting room) through the audience at the conclusion of the play. With her clothes faded and her face painted an unnatural ghostly white, she walked to the rear of the house, climbed a balcony rail, looked down at the spectators for several beats, then exited. From the spot of her disappearance an after-glow of blue light could be seen, and an eery electronic sound heard. The mysterious tone of the ending adequately captured an important element of Strauss's style. The naturalism of petty disputes between ex-lovers and the trivial family conversations which occupy much of the action of *Big and Little* is ultimately subordinate to the rhythm of the spiritual journey within Lotte.

In the crucial scene (the seventh of ten) of the play Lotte sits alone on stage, her only props being a chair and a gigantic book; she talks to herself, then to the book, the chair and ultimately God. Strauss displays the neurosis of this woman as it teeters at the edge of thorough-going madness. At the same time there is a passion here which is conspicuously absent from the rest of the play. Reciprocity seems possible with the inner voice, call it God or what you will, rather than with other human beings. In the headnote to *Big and Little* published for the Bochum production Strauss quotes from Edmund Jabès's *Book of Questions*: 'You are the one who writes and is written.' In scene 7 Lotte looks into an oversized book – 'The emptier it is the heavier it is' – and reads beyond her own mental and emotional crisis,

Things are dissolving.
We know that from science.
Or, if you will, the guest book.
Book losing script!

160

Or the mouth.
Mouth losing rouge.
Things are dissolving. . . .
Things that belong together
are sick of each other and fly apart.

Lotte's fear is quite real and complex. Her line, 'He makes
me feel so little', refers to all the men in her life, and also
to a God-figure she mentally wrestles The massive book
seems to erase itself; it also bleeds, and blood flows from
Lotte's back as the crisis deepens. The blood-letters spell
out the words 'Faithhopelove', as a mock reminder it
seems of a tradition of love and compassion which once
existed. Lotte's extreme state of emotion and the religious
overtones of the scene echo plays from the heyday of
German Expressionist Theatre when works by Toller (*The
Transformation*, subtitled 'A Man's Wrestling') and
Georg Kaiser (*From Morn To Midnight, Gas* and others)
showed individuals ecstatically searching for some
meaning or salvation, whether political or religious or
both, from their private agonies and sense of loss. *Big and
Little* is part of that tradition, but with the significant
difference that Strauss couches the very idea of salvation
ironically in the play as a whole.

Critics selected *Big and Little* as the best new play of the
1978 season. With the creation of the strong central
character of Lotte within an original set of stage images
Botho Strauss has made his most effective exploration to
date of the themes of alienation, loss of emotion and the
borders between 'normal' consciousness and spiritual/
imaginative awareness.

10
Conclusion

It is well known that there is no single theatre capital for German speaking countries equivalent to London or New York. Individual regions and cities, including Berlin, support numerous theatres which rise and fall in status depending on their current successes and the residency and leadership of innovative Intendants, directors, actors and dramaturgs.[1] Peter Stein at the Theater am Lehniner Platz (formerly the Schaubühne am Halleschen Ufer) and Claus Peymann in Bochum are only two directors' names to conjure with in the last ten years. Though the levels of subsidies at the various theatres are a constant source of debate, and though a tension exists between artistic freedom and public answerability in a state supported system, there is no doubt that German speaking countries are dedicated to the theatre as a cultural institution. For contemporary playwrights this does not automatically provide a bed of roses: in the seventies, Shakespeare and Brecht productions outstripped the total number of productions of all the plays by all the playwrights considered in this book by a ratio of six to one.[2] Nevertheless, the fact that the diversity of challenging plays, distinctly 'non-commercial products', currently being written in German can receive serious treatment by the best of directors, designers and actors is a sign of the healthy state of the German dramatic scene.

The Schauspielhaus Bochum in northern Germany, has made a concerted effort to foster new plays. Claus Peymann and a large staff arrived in Bochum in 1979 after a protracted struggle with authorities in Stuttgart over censorship (Peymann's view) and irresponsibility (the view of the cultural ministry). He was fired in the end ostensibly because of his open sympathy for a jailed terrorist, but the tone of productions (including a purportedly libellous play by Hochhuth about ex-Nazis in high government positions) at his Württenbürg Staatschauspiel had long been a source of irritation to his employers. In Bochum, under Peymann new productions are customarily accompanied by low cost published scripts including programme notes, interviews and related visual and literary material. Dramaturg Uwe Jens Jensen explained to me that the theatre guarantees a playwright the publication of his play as well as an advance fee and the normal royalties. It is their way of fostering new work. Bochum might decide it wants to do a production on a specific subject, in which case a suitable playwright is contacted (Hochhuth, say, on a sensitive political issue) and arrangements are made. Alternatively, if a given director and writer have an affinity for one another's work (as in the case of Peymann and Bernhard) the process is simply one of designating a premiere in the season when a new play has been written. There is also room for younger writers like Thomas Brasch to see their works staged, whether manuscripts are solicited or not. The writer in Bochum can expect an advance, a professional premiere and publication, all provided by the theatre.³ It took Franz Xaver Kroetz a while to achieve large scale productions, possibly because of his outspoken political views, though the network of lab spaces attached to large state theatres, and independent theatres like the Modernes Theater München, provided impressive premieres of the first plays. By the time the seventies had drawn to a close, however, Kroetz had garnered a larger audience than any other contemporary German language playwright, and was being produced by the best directors in Germany. The Schauspielhaus Bochum may be an exception in the extent of its encouragement of new work, but a glance at the season programme throughout Germany confirms that new plays are regularly staged at most theatres, despite the strong national commitment to the classical heritage.

The respect for serious new plays implicit in all this has its amusing side for a non-German observer. At a recent production of Strauss's *Big and Little* in Bochum I saw people in the audience following scripts while the play was in progress. This also occurred at a performance of George Tabori's adaptation of Hans Magnus Enzensberger's *The Sinking of the Titanic* which took place in a small circus tent on the outskirts of Munich, and which incorporated the lead clown from the family circus troupe in the production. When I asked performers and directors about this strange phenomenon they usually just shook their heads with a knowing resignation. George Froscher's answer to audiences in search of book-lessons in the theatre came in his Freies Theater München production of Handke's *Kaspar*. The number of 'script-readers' in that audience was particularly high, he explained, because of the difficulty of the text. Froscher decided to stage the play in a manner which Handke could only have approved of:

he instructed the 'Prompters' to impose their authority on the audience before beginning their assault on Kaspar. Orders were given to relinquish all books, which were duly collected and left in piles at the theatre entrance. The act of watching a play, with no text to hide behind, became for the audience the first in a series of confrontations in the process of socialization and consciousness which Handke presents in *Kaspar*.

Theater heute listed Dario Fo, Edward Bond, Athol Fugard and Harold Pinter as the most frequently performed foreign authors of the seventies, with a combined number of performances nearly as great as for the German language authors treated in this book. (Boulevard' playwrights like Alan Ayckbourne were discounted for the survey.) The choice of Fo, Bond and Fugard is indicative of the German theatres' preference for playwrights directly engaged in the political and social issues of the day. The same holds true of native writers, with Kroetz as the prime example. Even Bernhard, by his choice to debunk politics, and Handke in his self-conscious 'retreat' to Romanticism in the face of categorical issue-oriented thinking, partake in the 'art and engagement' debate which shapes the reception of new plays. One can see a relationship between the plays of Kroetz, based in naturalism but at their best straining to exceed its limitations, and the work of Arnold Wesker or David Storey. The simple rhythms of physical activity incorporated into the working class situations of *The Changing Room* or *The Contractor* have parallels in Kroetz's plays. And the broad range of themes and sympathies overlaps: problems in articulating vital emotional experiences and in counteracting alienation, especially among working class and lower middle class people. Where Kroetz differed in his early plays was in the

165

choice of material. I was present at a production of *Homeworker* (translated by Elizabeth Bond) at the Half Moon Theatre in London when several people became physically sick at the sight of the abortion attempt. The reality and the honesty which characterize the violence in Kroetz's early plays is perhaps closer to the work of another Englishman, Edward Bond. Since Peter Stein's production of *Saved* in the experimental space of the Münchner Kammerspiele in 1967 German theatres have shown great fascination for Bond's work. *Saved* was, incidentally, Peter Stein's directorial debut. Both the involvement as director and the tendency toward creating a genuine mythic stage poetry in recent works also make Bond comparable to Heiner Müller. As for Handke and Strauss, the obvious comparable figure in Britain is Tom Stoppard, whose plays are full of relationships between things 'which common sense would never have brought together'.[3] Their work derives from the modernist tradition of the surrealists, stresses the insufficiency of pure reason, and at its most effective possesses a genuine liberating humour.

In a recent panel discussion in New York a group of eminent American playwrights (Arthur Miller, Edward Albee, Lanford Wilson, David Mamet, and others) addressed the perennial question: 'What's Happening To The Serious American Playwright On Broadway?' The answer was not surprising: commercial pressures make survival rare. Even long-running plays have difficulty breaking even, thus making producers hesitant to invest in serious plays. And the once hoped-for alternative in regional theatre, according to the playwrights, is not what it might be. Plays are being written in surprising numbers in the United States, but they do not always have adequate avenues for professional production.[4] Relatively young playwrights like David Mamet, Sam Shepard and Thomas Babe are not so frequently produced in Germany, possibly because the social and political consciousness in American writers traditionally has been incorporated into private emotional and imagistic structures which do not suffer the sea change well. On the other hand American theatrical troupes which tour Germany (as the Bread and Puppet and San Francisco Mime Troupes have done) fare quite well.

The ways in which artists are influenced by different cultures and in turn exert influence on their contemporaries in other countries are difficult to define. The question is more complicated than simple tallies of numbers of productions would provide answers for. Peter Handke has expressed interest in The Bread and Puppet Theatre, and his fascination with American culture (the myths of the West; the Gangster, as translated by Hollywood; pop culture) is clear in his novels. An amusing example of the convoluted process of cultural absorption occurred in Bruno Bayen's production of Handke's *They Are Dying Out*. Act II opened with strains of Mozart over the loudspeakers, while the 'businessman-poet' Quitt stood next to a Mercedes-Benz limousine. The music then changed to a country-western version of Brecht/Weill's 'Oh Moon of Alabama', a song originally written in English by a German Marxist poet at a time when 'Jazz Age' America was a powerful influence on European culture. In his play, of course, Handke treats just this conundrum of the man in search of 'un-influenced' thought and feeling: the 'Alabama Song' joke reinforces the complexity (and perhaps absurdity) of the issue in the late twentieth century. The processes of communication have speeded up to such a degree that the search for influences seems futile. For Kroetz, who sees himself writing in a tradition shared by the Arthur Miller of *Death of a Salesman* and *All My Sons*, the American cultural influence is different. The number of plays he has written which call for a radio in the background playing the AFN (American Forces Network) station indicates clearly that from his point of view his generation's thoughts have been 'colonized' by the U.S. long after the 'de-Nazification' period. His efforts to revitalize a pre-Nazi folk play, derived from Nestroy, Fleisser, and Horváth, are implicitly in answer to that powerful American influence.

When I spoke to George Tabori's troupe the question of influence and reception was brought home to me in an enlightening manner. George Tabori, one of the more innovative directors in Germany today, operates on the fringes of the subsidized theatre structure, retaining his own troupe as an experimental wing of state or city supported theatres. Despite difficulties with various theatres, Tabori has managed to produce important pieces in the seventies, including one about his mother, a Hungarian Jewess, who escaped the gas chamber (*My Mother's Courage*, 1979). One of the actors in Tabori's troupe is the American Murray Levy, who candidly expressed to me his contempt for most of the state supported theatre in Germany's culture industry. (I asked him whether he knew who Franz Xaver Kroetz was, and he said he did not.) Levy had played Vladimir in the famous Free Southern Theatre production of *Godot* which toured the American South in the sixties, and he was an original member of Schumann's Bread and Puppet Theatre, at the time when the company was praised, along with other troupes like the Living Theatre in Europe in the late sixties. Levy, working with Tabori in a company which shows clear similarities to the work of the Living Theatre, The Open Theatre and others, is a sign of a real connection between two theatre traditions. As I write these lines I read in the *New York Times* that one of the foremost American directors of the seventies, Richard Foreman, has just opened a production of Botho Strauss's *Trilogie des Wiedersehens* at the Public Theatre in New York (translated as *Three Acts of Recognition* by Sophie Wilkins). The cross fertilization is there, constantly, even if those who are involved are not always aware of it. I hope this book can be part of the process of keeping the cultural channels open.

The End Of An Era? is the title the Soho Poly Theatre of London used for its 1982 season of German plays, which included Kroetz's *Neither Fish Nor Fowl*, Bernhard's *Eve of Retirement*, and Müller's *The Mission*. As a headnote for its brochure the theatre quoted Heiner Müller:

For anything to come something must go.
The first shape of hope is fear.
The first appearance of the new is terror.

The feeling that things are changing in a manner beyond understanding in divided Germany and the world at large leads to the dramatic expressions of blind conflict and alienation in Müller and Brasch. For Kroetz the 'little man' sees himself caught up in large hostile processes, his hope for changing his circumstances real but not great.

One can trace a lineage from Büchner's *Woyzeck*, through Brecht's *Galy Gay* (*Man is Man*) to Brasch's *Rotter*. For Rainer Werner Fassbinder, whose death in 1982 added a particularly sombre note to the theme of an era at its end, vexed 'little people' were also a recurring subject. A sign of a continuing tradition is Fassbinder's thirteen part 1980 television series based on Alfred Döblin's *Berlin Alexanderplatz* about the ex-convict Franz Biberkopf in the chaos of Berlin in the twenties. The later naturalists' serious interest in social realities and the plight of the masses continues into the contemporary theatre. Kroetz draws on the folk plays of Horváth and Fleisser as resources. Müller and Brasch utilize more expressionistic techniques in their recent pieces, but all of them, as Brecht had done, emphasize the need for artists to be engaged in the pressing issues of the day. Their mission is to shape the new era, however differently each one perceives the 'era' and the process of shaping it.

As for the writers less 'realistically' oriented, there is Bernhard whose cynicism has its roots in the last call for 'significant' change, one that was to last 1000 years. Strauss and Handke respond to the demise of an era by seeking inner strength, and place their faith in art itself. It is perhaps fitting to conclude with a few remarks on Handke's most recent effort, *Among the Villages* (1981). In it, an old woman, a voice from the village, bids the potential poet/saviour Gregor: 'Make each one of your words as clear as a bark and show the barbed wire inside your mouth.' Handke's advice to actors for this play is: 'Here *I* stand. – All are right. – After the concluding lines, keep playing. – Inner irony.' By means of the self, and through the irony, comes a strength. Within a structure of massive carefully carefully wrought monologues, some as long as fourteen pages, combined with individual and group chanting, curious bits of mime (e.g., one in which three 'shaven washed, combed . . . transformed' construction workers act out the behaviour of 'Herr Lawyer' on a visit to 'Herr Architect' while a fourth describes the scene), and a climactic religiose sermon on Nature, Art and the value of Self by a character named Nova, through whom 'the spirit of the new age' speaks, Handke continues to elaborate on themes he first treated dramatically in *They Are Dying Out*, and which have preoccupied him steadily since 1979 in *Slow Homecoming* (1979), *The Teachings of the Sainte-Victoire* (1980), *A Child's Story* (1981). Together with *Among the Villages*, he has referred to these last works as a tetralogy, which should be given the general title 'Slow Homecoming'.

Among the Villages makes use of parody and irony, though more sparingly than the previous plays, especially in the lengthy speeches which come across as rhetorical flights of the author's own. 'Character' still has no place in Handke's drama. The conflict in *Among the Villages*, such as it is, exists between the longing of an artist (a writer: 'Yeah, talk, that he could do', his parents said) named Gregor to preserve what he can of natural purity in the face of 'civilized progress', and the desire of his siblings, a trained craftsman turned manual labourer, Hans, and Sophie, a shopgirl, to achieve independence through the cash value of the family house and land which the older Gregor has inherited. They want to mortgage the property and use the money to establish a business for Sophie. Though Gregor relinquishes his claim in the end, the sense of the whole is that this 'man with the [holy?] writ', and Nova, who accompanies him, have brought about the opportunity for people to transform themselves, to recognize joy as the 'only legitimate power' and to see artists as those capable of 'creating the people'. As all the figures in the play utter a similarly inspired language they are all potentially artists. Certainly the yearning for something higher is there, and the capability. The idea is not unrelated to Beuys's thought for the 'free university', referred to in the introduction of this book. Handke goes a distance toward fantasizing out of existence all of the conflicts (class, family, etc.) under a generalized Romantic credo in *Among the Villages*. The play ends in front of the ancient village cemetery where Nova gradually ascends a ladder behind a wall while she delivers her speech to intensified strains of caravan music. The rest of the people on stage place masks shaped from the forest greenery on their faces, and watch as Nova places a crown on the head of Hans's son. The boy had performed as mock-acolyte just prior to this, rattling the coins in his money-box to accompany his father's forlorn chant ('we are not on the path of error, but on no path at all') and grotesque dance of 'forsaken humanity'. In the end, the people are transformed; the worker's son is the new poet. Handke's poetic fantasy is the other side of the coin to the 'realist playwrights' analyses; all of them agree to the need for fundamental change.

Notes

1. Introduction

1. *Das Theater der siebziger Jahre* (Stuttgart, 1980), p. 336.
2. C. D. Innes, *Modern German Drama* (New York, 1979), 'Introduction' and *passim*.
3. The scene is printed in the March 1978 issue of *Theater heute*.
4. Günter Wallraff, *Ihr da oben – wir da unten* (*You Up There, We Down Here*) (Hamburg, 1976), p. 63.
5. Caroline Tisdall, *Josef Beuys* (New York, 1979), p. 282.
6. Ibid, p. 182.

2. The Playwrights

1. Tisdall, *Beuys*, p. 280.
2. Ibid., p. 228.
3. Written c. 1977, 'Sozialismus aus Liebe zum Vernünftigen' ('Socialism Out of a Love For Reason') is part of the collection *Warum Ich Marxist Bin* (*Why I Am A Marxist*), ed. Fritz J. Raddatz, (Frankfurt am Main, 1980) pp. 31–51.
4. Speech delivered at the Mannheim General Assembly of the German Communist Party, quoted in *Unsere Zeit*, 9 May 1980.

5. See the introduction to Peter Iden, *Die Schaubühne am Halleschen Ufer 1970–1979* (München, 1979).

6. 'The Aporias of the Avant-Garde', in *The Consciousness Industry, On Literature, Politics and the Media*, selected with a Postscript by Michael Roloff (New York, 1974), p. 40.

3. Kroetz and Handke: A Comparison

1. June Schlueter refers to Sartre's notion of 'ocular assault' in this context in *The Plays and Novels of Peter Handke* (Pittsburgh, 1981), p. 52.

4. Handke: Short Pieces and 'Kaspar'

1. Interview with Heinz Ludwig Arnold (1975), in *Text + Kritik* (24/24a) (München, 1978), p. 28.

2. Interview with Judith Cook, published in her book, *Directors' Theatre* (London, 1974), reprinted in Ronald Hayman, *Theatre and Anti-Theatre* (Oxford, 1979), p. 197.

3. *After Babel* (London, 1975), p. 474.

5. Handke: 'The Ride Across Lake Constance' and 'They Are Dying Out'

1. *Letters from Ludwig Wittgenstein* with a Memoir by P. Engelmann, (London, 1967), p. 7.

2. Interview with Heinz Ludwig Arnold (1975), in *Text + Kritik* (24/24a), ed. Heinz Ludwig Arnold, (München, 1978), p. 28. In a later interview with June Schlueter (1979) he speaks of a new play: 'I have a certain vision of a play, that would be one person who addressed the people for three hours. . . . Everything else in the theatre strikes me as tricky – for me.' June Schlueter, *The Plays and Novels of Peter Handke* (Pittsburgh, 1981), p. 175.

6. Kroetz, Fassbinder and Drama for the Masses

1. The notes on *Eight Hours* were provided by Ben Brewster,

former editor of *Sight and Sound* at a three-day conference on German cinema at North London Polytechnic, 1975. Further references to the series can be found in *Rainer Werner Fassbinder* (Reihe Film 2, Hanser) (München, 1979).

7. Kroetz: The Search For New Forms

1. See Rolf-Peter Carl, *Franz Xaver Kroetz* (Munich, 1978), pp. 93, ff.

8. Voices from East Germany: Heiner Müller and Thomas Brasch

1. Interview with Reinhold Grimm and Jost Hermand in *Basis: Jahrbuch für deutsche Gegenwartsliteratur.* Band 6. (Frankfurt am Main, 1976), p. 56.
2. Ibid., p. 52.
3. Carl Weber, 'Heiner Müller. The Despair and the Hope', *Performing Arts Journal*, 12 (New York, 1980), p. 140.
4. André Wirth. 'Errinerung an eine Revolution: sado-masochistisch', *Theater heute*, 1 (Berlin, 1980), p. 8.
5. Ibid., p. 6.

9. Private Visions: Thomas Bernhard and Botho Strauss

1. Interview with André Müller (1979) printed in Schauspielhaus Bochum programme and text of *The World Reformer* (16) (Bochum, 1980), p. 149.
2. Georg Hensel, review of *Before Retirement* in *Frankfurter Allgemeine Zeitung*, 2 July 1979, reprinted in *Das Theater der siebziger Jahre* (Stuttgart, 1980), p. 283.
3. Compare this to Jean Genet's remark: 'The world has never contained more than a single man. He exists quite completely inside each one of us. Therefore he is ourselves. Each of us is the other person and all the others.' Quoted by Ronald Hayman, *Theatre and Anti-Theatre* (New York, 1979), p. 72.
4. 'Ästhetik des Verlustes', *Theater 1976* (*Theater heute* annual), (Berlin), p. 104.

10. Conclusion

1. See Michael Patterson, *German Theatre Today* (London, 1976) for details on the theatre system in Germany.

2. *Theater heute* (6) June 1980, p. 74. Dieter Hadamczik lists the following number of performances for the seventies in West Germany and Berlin: Brecht and Shakespeare about 12,000 each; Bernhard 365; Brasch 121; Kroetz 2,784; Müller 458; Strauss 369. Handke was not considered among the ten most important writers. Other German language playwrights were: Volker Braun 55; Dieter Forte 663; Ulrich Planzdorf 1,511; Gerlind Reinshagen 442; Peter Weiss 981. The four most performed foreign authors were Edward Bond 519; Dario Fo 1,174; Athol Fugard 567; Harold Pinter 1,831.

3. Ronald Hayman, *Theatre and Anti-Theatre* (New York, 1979), p. 141.

4. Quoted by Ronald Hayman, *Theatre and Anti-Theatre*, (New York, 1979), p. 141.

5. American Society For Theatre Research Convention at Lincoln Center, New York, November 1981. The most upsetting worry expressed by the panel was the trend of producers with film interests increasingly putting their money behind regional productions on the speculative basis of their becoming profitable movie 'products'. The value of the play as such thus takes second place to its pure investment potential. Arthur Miller explained that good plays are around, as the Dramatist Play Service assured him, but do not get adequate productions.

Bibliography

PETER HANDKE

A. Play Collections

Publikumsbeschimpfung und andere Sprechstücke. (Frankfurt am Main: Suhrkamp, 1966) [*Offending The Audience, Prophecy, Self-Accusation*]

Prosa Gedichte Theaterstücke Hörspiel Aufsätze. (Frankfurt am Main: Suhrkamp, 1969) [Radio play, stories, poems, essays, *Offending The Audience, My Foot My Tutor*]

Stücke 1. (Frankfurt am Main: Suhrkamp, 1972) [*Offending The Audience, Prophecy, Self-Accusation, Calling For Help, Kaspar*]

Stücke 2. (Frankfurt am Main: Suhrkamp, 1973) [*My Foot My Tutor, Quodlibet, The Ride Across Lake Constance*]

Der Rand der Wörter: Erzählungen Gedichte Stücke. Ed. Heinz F. Schafroth. (Stuttgart: Philipp Reclam 1975). [Stories, poems, *Prophecy, Calling For Help, Quodlibet*]

B. Other Dramatic Works

Hörspiel Nr. 2, 3, und 4: (Frankfurt am Main: Verlag der Autoren, 1970) [Radio plays]

177

Chronik der laufenden Ereignisse. (Frankfurt am Main: Verlag der Autoren, 1970) [*A Chronicle of Events in Progress*: filmed by Handke in 1968–69]

Die Unvernünftigen sterben aus (*They Are Dying Out*), (Frankfurt am Main: Suhrkamp, 1973)

Wind und Meer: Vier Hörspiele (*Wind and Sea: Four Radio Plays*), (Frankfurt am Main: Suhrkamp, 1970)

Falsche Bewegung (*False Move*). (Frankfurt am Main: Suhrkamp, 1975.) [Screenplay for Wim Wenders' film]

Über die Dörfer (*Among the Villages*), (Frankfurt am Main: Surhkamp, 1982)

C. Novels/Fiction

Die Hornissen (*The Hornets*) (Frankfurt am Main: Suhrkamp, 1966)

Der Hausierer (*The Peddler*) (Frankfurt am Main: Suhrkamp, 1967)

Die Angst des Tormanns beim Elfmeter (*The Goalie's Anxiety at the Penalty Kick*). (Frankfurt am Main: Suhrkamp, 1970) [Also a film by Peter Handke and Wim Wenders]

Der Kurze Brief zum langen Abschied (*Short Letter, Long Farewell*). (Frankfurt am Main: Suhrkamp, 1972.) [Also a film by Herbert Vesely]

Wünschloses Unglück (*A Sorrow Beyond Dreams*). (Salzburg: Residenz, 1972)

Die Stünde der wahren Empfindung (*A Moment of True Feeling*). (Frankfurt am Main: Suhrkamp, 1975)

Die linkshändige Frau (*The Left Handed Woman*), (Frankfurt am Main: Suhrkamp, 1976.) [Also a film by Peter Handke]

Langsame Heimkehr (*Slow Homecoming*), (Frankfurt am Main: Suhrkamp, 1979)

D. Other Works

Kindergeschichte (*A Child's Story*), (Frankfurt am Main: Suhrkamp, 1981)

Begrüssung des Aufsichtsrats: Prosatexte (*Greeting the Board of Directors: Prose*), (Salzburg: Residenz, 1967)

Bibliography

Deutsche Gedichte (*German Poems*), (Frankfurt am Main: Euphorion, 1969)

Die Innenwelt der Aussenwelt der Innenwelt (*The Innerworld of the Outerworld of the Innerworld*), (Frankfurt am Main: Suhrkamp, 1969). [Poetry]

Ich bin ein Bewohner des Elfenbeinturms (*I am a Resident of the Ivory Tower*), (Frankfurt: Suhrkamp, 1972). [Essays]

Als das Wünschen noch geholfen hat (*When Wishing Still Helped*), (Frankfurt: Suhrkamp, 1974). [Poetry]

Das Gewicht der Welt: Ein Journal (November 1975–Marz 1977) (*The Weight of the World: A Journal*), (Salzburg: Residenz, 1977). [Journal/fiction]

Die Lehre der Sainte-Victoire (*The Teaching of The Sainte-Victoire*), (Frankfurt am Main: Suhrkamp, 1980). [Prose]

E. Translations

1. Plays

Kaspar and Other Plays. Trans. Michael Roloff. (New York: Farrar, Straus and Giroux, 1969.) [*Kaspar, Offending The Audience, Self-Accusation*]

Offending The Audience and Self-Accusation. Trans. Michael Roloff, (London: Methuen, 1971)

The Ride Across Lake Constance and Other Plays. Trans. Michael Roloff, (New York: Farrar, Straus and Giroux, 1976). [*Prophecy, Calling For Help, My Foot My Tutor, Quodlibet, The Ride Across Lake Constance, They Are Dying Out*]

2. Novels

Three by Peter Handke. Trans. Michael Roloff and Ralph Manheim. (New York: Farrar, Straus and Giroux, 1977.) [*The Goalie's Anxiety at the Penalty Kick; Short Letter, Long Farewell; A Sorrow Beyond Dreams*]

Two Novels by Peter Handke. Trans. Ralph Manheim. (New York: Farrar, Straus and Giroux, 1979.) [*A Moment of True Feeling; The Left-Handed Woman*]

3. Other

The Innerworld of The Outerworld of The Innerworld. Trans.

Michael Roloff. (New York: The Seabury Press, 1974.)
[Poetry bilingual]
Nonsense and Happiness. Trans. Michael Roloff. (New York:
Urizen, 1976.) [Poetry, bilingual]
Slow Homecoming (Langsame Heimkehr) and *The Weight of
The World (Das Gewicht der Welt)* forthcoming from Farrar,
Straus and Giroux.

FRANZ XAVER KROETZ

A. Play Collections

Gesammelte Stücke. (Frankfurt am Main: Suhrkamp, 1975)
[*Game Crossing, Home-Worker, Pig-Headed, Men's
Business, Dear Fritz, Stallerhof, Ghost Train, Request
Concert, Michi's Blood, Lienz: City of the Dolomites, Upper
Austria, Maria Magdalena, Munich's Children*]. The last four
are also available in a 1972 Suhrkamp collection.
Weitere Aussichten . . . Ein Lesebuch, ed. by Thomas Thieringer
with Wolfgang Schuch and Jochen Ziller. (Köln: Kiepenheuer
and Witsch, 1976). [Filmscripts: *The Accident, The Gentle
Kind*; Radio Plays: *Inclusive, Quick Recovery, Balance Sheet,
The Choice For Life*; Plays: *Pennies From Heaven, The Nest,
Future Prospects, Voyage to Happiness, Home, Agnes
Bernauer*; *Help, I'm Getting Married!*, interviews; essays;
polemical writings]
*Mensch Meier, Der stramme Max, Wer durchs Laub geht . . .
Drei neue Stücke.* (Frankfurt am Main: Suhrkamp, 1979).
[*Mensch Meier, Big Max, He Who Through The Foliage
Wanders*]
Ein Lesebuch (A Reader), (Reinbeck: Rowohlt, 1982)

B. Selected Other Works

*Chiemgauer Gschichten. Bayerische Menschen erzählen (Stories
From The Chiemgau: Bavarians Speak).* (Köln: Kiepenheuer
und Witsch, 1977) [interviews, reportage]
Der Mondscheinknecht (Slave of the Moon). (Frankfurt am
Main: Suhrkamp, 1981.) [Novel]

Bibliography

C. Translations

Farmyard and Four Plays, with an introduction by Richard Gilman, (*Request Concert*, tr. Peter Sander; *Farmyard* [*Stallerhof*], tr. Michael Roloff and Jack Gelber; *Michi's Blood*, tr. Michael Roloff and Denise Gordon; *A Man, A Dictionary* [revision of *Men's Business*], tr. by Michael Roloff and Carl Weber.) (New York: Urizen, 1976)

Stallerhof, tr. Katherine Hehn, in *Bauer, Fassbinder, Handke, Kroetz.* (London: Eyre Methuen, 1977)

HEINER MÜLLER

A. Play Collections

Geschichten aus der Produktion 1. (Berlin: Rotbuch Verlag, 1974) [*The Scab, Correction, The Work Site, Herakles*, poetry, prose, interviews, materials related to plays]

Geschichten aus der Produktion 2. (Berlin: Rotbuch Verlag, 1974) [*The Tractor, Prometheus, Cement*, poetry, prose]

Die Umsiedlerin oder Das Leben auf dem Lande. (Berlin: Rotbuch Verlag, 1975) [*The Battle, Medea-Play, The Peasants* (*Evacué*), poetry]

Theater-Arbeit. (Berlin: Rotbuch Verlag, 1975.) [*God of Good Luck, Dragon Opera* (Paul Dessau opera), *Horizons, Women's Comedy*, essays on theatre]

Germania Tod in Berlin. (Berlin: Rotbuch Verlag, 1977.) [*Germania Death in Berlin*, poetry, prose, visual material]

Mauser. (Berlin: Rotbuch Verlag, 1978.) [*Philoctetes, Oedipus Commentary, The Horatians, Mauser, Hamletmachine*, materials related to plays]

Kopien. 3 Versuche, Shakespeare zu töten (*Three Efforts at Killing Shakespeare*), (Frankfurt am Main: Suhrkamp, 1977.) [*As You Like It, Horizons*]

Shakespeare Factory 2. (Frankfurt am Main: Suhrkamp) [*Macbeth, Polyp, Hamlet*]

Quartett. (Frankfurt am Main: Verlag der Autoren, 1981)

B. Translations

Cement (*Zement*) translated by Helen Fehervary, Sue-Ellen Case, Marc D. Silberman, *New German Critique*, Supplement to Issue No. 16 (Winter 1979), Milwaukee, Wisconsin, U.S.A.

THOMAS BRASCH

A. Plays

Die Argentinische Nacht (*The Argentine Night*), (Frankfurt am Main: Verlag der Autoren, 1977)

Der Papiertiger (*The Paper Tiger*) in *Spectaculum 26.* (Frankfurt am Main: Suhrkamp, 1977), pp. 7–31

Lovely Rita in *Spectaculum 28.* (Frankfurt am Main: Suhrkamp, 1978), pp. 59–79

Rotter und weiter. Ein Tagebuch, ein Stück, eine Aufführung (*Rotter and More: A Diary, A Play, A Production*). (Frankfurt am Main: Suhrkamp, 1978)

Lieber Georg. Ein Eis-Kunst-Läufer-Drama aus dem Vorkrieg (*Dear George. A Show Skating Drama From The Pre-War Days*). (Schauspielhaus Bochum, 1980).

B. Other Works

Poesiealbum 89, ed. Bernd Jentzsch. (East Berlin: Neues Leben, 1975.) [Poetry]

Vor den Vätern sterben die Söhne (*Sons Dying Before Their Fathers*). (Berlin: Rotbuch, 1977) [Stories]

Kargo 32. Versuch auf einem untergehenden Schiff aus der eigenen Haut zu kommen (*Cargo 32. An Attempt to Get Out of One's Skin While The Ship is Sinking*). (Frankfurt am Main: Suhrkamp, 1977) [*Lovely Rita*, dramatic sketches, prose, poetry, photographs]

Stockfremd. Auszug aus einem Versuch die Sprache des Staatsbürgers als Dichtung zu lesen (*Strange. Excerpt From an Attempt to Read the Language of the Citizens as Poetry*) in the Photo Book, *Im anderen Deutschland*, (Berlin: Artemis Verlag, 1979)

Bibliography

Der Schöne 27. September, (Frankfurt am Main: Suhrkamp, 1980). [Poetry]
Engel aus Eisen (Iron Angel), (Frankfurt am Main: Suhrkamp, 1981). [Screenplay]
Gladow. (Frankfurt am Main: Suhrkamp, 1981)

THOMAS BERNHARD

A. Plays

1. Plays published by Suhrkamp, Frankfurt am Main:
Ein Fest für Boris (A Feast for Boris, 1970); *Der Ignorant und der Wahnsinnige (The Ignoramus and The Madman*, 1971; *Die Jagdgesellschaft (The Hunting Party*, 1974); *Die Macht der Gewohnheit (The Force of Habit*, 1975); *Der Präsident (The President*, 1975); *Die Berühmten (The Famous Ones*, 1976); *Minetti* (1977); *Immanuel Kant* (1978); *Vor dem Ruhestand (Before Retirement*, 1979); Suhrkamp has also issued photographs and a double album recording of Bernhard Minetti in the premiere of *Der Weltverbesserer* (1980).

2. Other Plays:
Die Rosen der Einöde, Fünf Sätze für Ballet, Stimmen und Orchester (Roses of Solitude, Five Compositions for Ballet, Voices and Orchestra) (Frankfurt am Main: S. Fischer, 1959) and *Der Berg (The Mountain*, subtitled *A Play for Marionettes as Humans or Humans as Marionettes*) in *Literatur and Kritik* 5, 1970. At the time of going to press, the cabaret sketches, *Dramolette* (1981), and *Ein Deutscher Mittagstisch (Dinner in Germany*, 1979) were not published.

B. Major Fiction

Frost. Frankfurt am Main: Insel, 1963; *Amras.* Frankfurt am Main: Insel, 1964; *Verstörung (Derangement).* Frankfurt am Main: Insel, 1967; *Prosa (Prose).* Frankfurt am Main: Suhrkamp, 1967; *Ungenach.* Frankfurt am Main: Suhrkamp, 1968; *Watten.* Frankfurt am Main: Suhrkamp, 1969; *An der Baumgrenze (At The Edge of The Forest).* Salzburg: Residenz, 1969; *Das Kalkwerk (The Lime Works).* Frankfurt

am Main: Suhrkamp, 1970; *Midland in Stilfs.* Frankfurt am
Main: Suhrkamp, 1971; *Gehen (Going).* Frankfurt am Main:
Suhrkamp, 1971; *Der Italiener (The Italian).* Salzburg:
Residenz, 1971; *Der Kulterer (The Cultist).* Salzburg:
Residenz, 1974; *Korrektur (The Correction).* Frankfurt am
Main: Suhrkamp, 1975; *Die Ursache. Eine Andeutung (The
Cause. An Indication)* Salzburg: Residenz, 1975; *Der
Wetterfleck (Spot of Weather).* Erzählungen. Stuttgart:
Reclam, 1976; *Der Keller. Eine Entziehung (The Cellar, A
Withdrawal).* Salzburg: Residenz, 1976; *Der Atem. Eine
Entscheidung (Breath. A Decision).* Salzburg: Residenz, 1978;
Ja (Yes). Frankfurt am Main: Suhrkamp, 1978; *Der
Stimmenimitator (The Mimic).* Frankfurt am Main:
Suhrkamp, 1978; *Ein Kind (A Child).* Frankfurt am Main:
Suhrkamp, 1982.

C. Translations

1. Plays

The Force of Habit (Die Macht der Gewohnheit). Translated by
Neville and Stephen Plaice. (London: Heinemann Educational
for the National Theatre, 1976)
The President and *Eve of Retirement (Der Präsident* and *Vor
dem Ruhestand).* Translated by Gitta Honegger. (New York:
Performing Arts Journal Publications, 1982)

2. Novels

Gargoyles (Verstörung, literally *Derangement).* Translated by
Richard and Clara Winston. (New York: Knopf, 1970)
The Lime Works (Das Kalkwerk). Translated by Sophie Wilkins.
(New York: Random House, 1973)
Correction (Korrektur). Translated by Sophie Wilkins. (New
York: Knopf, 1979)

BOTHO STRAUSS

A. Plays

Die Hypochonder; Bekannte Gesichter, gemischte Gefühle. Zwei

Bibliography

Theaterstücke (*The Hypochondriacs*; *Familiar Faces, Mixed Feelings*). (München: Hanser, 1979)
Trilogie des Wiedersehens (*A Trilogy of Reunions*). (München: Hanser, 1976)
Gross und Klein (*Big and Little*). (München: Hanser, 1978)

B. Fiction

Marlenes Schwester. Zwei Erzählungen. (München: Hanser, 1975)
Die Widmung. Eine Erzählung (*Devotion*). (München: Hanser, 1977)
Rumor (*Rumour*). (München: Hanser, 1980)
Paare Passanten (*Passing Couples*). (München: Hanser, 1981)

C. Translations

Big and Little (*Gross und Klein*), translated by Anne Cattaneo. (New York: Farrar, Straus and Giroux, 1979)
Devotion (*Die Widmung*), translated by Sophie Wilkins. (New York: Farrar, Straus and Giroux, 1979)

Secondary Sources in English

Chambers, Helen. 'Thomas Bernhard Checklist' in *Theatrefacts* Vol. III, 1976, no. 4, pp. 2–11.
Hayman, Ronald (ed.) *The German Theatre*. (London: Wolff, 1975).
———. *Theatre and Anti-Theatre*. (New York: Oxford University Press, 1979).
Hern, Nicholas. *Peter Handke, Theatre and Anti-Theatre*. (London: Wolff, 1970).
Huettich, H. G. *Theatre in the Planned Society. Contemporary Drama in the German Democratic Republic*. (Chapel Hill: University of North Carolina Press, 1978).
Innes, Christopher. *Modern German Drama. A Study in Form*. (Cambridge: Cambridge University Press, 1979).
Modern Drama. 'Special German Issue'. Vol. XXIII, 1981,

no. 4. (Articles on Handke, Bernhard, Müller, Kroetz, others; includes bibliography).

Patterson, Michael. *German Theatre Today.* (London: Pitman, 1976).

Rorrison, Hugh. 'Franz Xaver Kroetz Checklist' in *Theatrefacts* Vol. III, 1976, no. 2, pp. 2–16.

Rayns, Tony (ed.) *Fassbinder.* (London: British Film Institute, 1976) revised, 1981.

Schlueter, June. *The Plays and Novels of Peter Handke.* (Pittsburgh; University of Pittsburgh Press, 1981).

Shaw, Leroy R. (ed.) *The German Theatre Today.* A Symposium (Austin, Texas: University of Texas Press, 1963).

Thomas, R. Hinton, and Keith Bullivant. *Literature in Upheaval. West German Writers and the Challenge of the 1960's.* (Manchester: Manchester University Press, 1974).

Secondary Sources in German

The monthly journal *Theater heute* is the best source of current information on German language theatre. Annual special volumes (*Theater: Jahrbuch der Zeitschrift Theater heute*) provide extended essays, overviews and bibliographies. The 1980 annual summarizes important events in theatre and drama since 1960. *Theater der Zeit* is the equivalent East German journal. Since bibliographies in German on all but Thomas Brasch and Botho Strauss would run to numerous pages the following is limited to easily accessible monographs and series:

Arnold, Heinz Ludwig. *Text and Kritik*, München: this series which contains factual information, interviews and articles includes volumes on Peter Handke (1978), Thomas Bernhard (1974), Franz Xaver Kroetz (1978), and Heiner Müller (1981).

The *Autorenbücher* series published by C. H. Beck, München, includes R. Nagele and R. Voris, *Peter Handke* (no. 8) 1978; Rolf-Peter Carl, *Franz Xaver Kroetz* (no. 10) 1978; Bernard Sorg, *Thomas Bernhard* (no. 7) 1977. Each contains a select bibliography.

Suhrkamp, Frankfurt am Main has published the critical collections, Michael Scharang (ed.), *Über Peter Handke*, 1972 and Anneliese Botond (ed.) *Über Thomas Bernhard*, 1970.

Index

187

Index

Herzog, Werner 66
Hermann, Karl-Ernst 104, 107, 159
Heym, Georg 24
Hiob, Hanne, *see* Brecht, Hanne Hiob
Hochhuth, Rolf 19, 42, 163
Hoffmannsthal, Hugo von 151
Holz, Jürgen 129
Horvath, Ödön von 19, 70, 96, 111, 168, 169

Ibsen, Henrik: *Peer Gynt* 25, 136, 150
Iden, Peter 25, 26, 75
Innes, Christopher D. 4
Ionesco, Eugène 3, 57

Jabès, Edmund 160
Jean Paul (Johann Paul Friedrich Richter) 11
Jensen, Uwe Jens 163
Jessner, Leopold 146

Kafka, Franz 130
Kaiser, Georg 161
Kaspar Hauser 14, 64–5, 66, 68
Kohl, Helmut 44, 45
Kroetz, Franz Xaver 3–26 *passim*, 46, 47, 91–113 *passim*, 165; plays: *Agnes Bernauer* 108–11; *Big Max* 98, 104; *Choice for Life* 29, 43–7; *Dear Fritz* 94; *Future Prospects* 50, 98; *Game Crossing* 93; *Ghost Train* 47–52; *Global Interest* 112; *He Who Through the Foliage Wanders* 92; *Homework(er)* 20, 166; *Lienz, City of the Dolomites* 112–16; *Man a Dictionary* 92; *Maria Magdalena* 108; *Men's Business* 92; *Mensch Meier* 19, 95, 97–114;

Munich's Children 112; *Neither Fish Nor Fowl* 21, 104–7, 169; *Nest* 93, 95–8, 150; *Pennies From Heaven* 112–13; *Pig-Headed* 94; *Request Concert* 18, 20, 26, 51; *Stallerhof (Farmyard)* 20, 29, 47–52, 91; *Upper Austria* 93, 95–8; other works: *Adam Deigl and the Authorities* 93, 95; *Chiemgauer Gschichten* 100, 103, and new theatre/literature 18, 19, 89, 164–8

Lessing, Gotthold Ephraim 81
Levy, Murray 168
Living Theatre 168

Mamet, David 166
Mann, Thomas 140
Marcuse, Herbert 130
Marxism 4, 12, 20, 22, 87, 92, 110, 117, 167
Meinhof, Ulrike 5, 6, 10
Miller, Arthur 92, 166–8
Minetti, Bernhard 144, 146–8
Modernes Theater München 101, 164
Müller, Heiner 4, 14, 22–4, 120–2, 126, 129, 170; *Cement* 122–5, 126–7; *Construction* 118; *Farmers* 118; *Germania Death in Berlin* 23; *Hamletmachine* 127–8; *Mauser* 120–2; *Mission* 128–31, 169; *Philoctetes* 119–20; *Scab* 118–19; *Tractor* 118; *Women's Comedy* 125–6; and new theatre/literature: 27, 128, 140, 149, 166
Müller, Inge 125
Münchner Kammerspiele 166
Münzner, Wolf 115

189

New German Dramatists